Of Texas Rivers and Texas Art

RIVER BOOKS, SPONSORED BY

Andrew Sansom, General Editor

Of Texas Rivers & Texas Art

ANDREW SANSOM AND WILLIAM E. REAVES

TEXAS A&M UNIVERSITY PRESS COLLEGE STATION

First edition

This paper meets the requirements
of ANSI/NISO Z39.48-1992
(Permanence of Paper).
Binding materials have been
chosen for durability.
Manufactured in China
by Everbest Printing Co.
through FCI Print Group

Title page art: David Caton, *Fast Waters of Rio Frio at Garner State Park*

A list of the titles in this series appears at the end of the book.

LIBRARY OF CONGRESS CATALOGING-IN-PUBLICATION DATA

Names: Sansom, Andrew, compiler, author. | Reaves, William E., compiler, author. | Container of (work): Sansom, Andrew. Rivers and people.
Title: Of Texas rivers and Texas art / Andrew Sansom and William E. Reaves.
Other titles: River books (Series)
Description: First edition. | College Station: Texas A&M University Press, [2017] | Series: River books | Includes index.
Identifiers: LCCN 2016038037 (print) | LCCN 2016040012 (ebook) | ISBN 9781623495343 (cloth: alk. paper) | ISBN 9781623495350 (ebook)
Subjects: LCSH: Rivers—Texas—Pictorial works. | Stream conservation—Texas. | Rivers in art. | Painting, American—Texas—21st century.
Classification: LCC F392.A17 S26 2017 (print) | LCC F392.A17 (ebook) | DDC 976.4—dc23
LC record available at https://lccn.loc.gov/2016038037

CONTENTS

Acknowledgments vii
Rivers and People, by Andrew Sansom 1
Tracing the River as Muse in the Lone Star Landscape,
by William E. Reaves 19

Featured Art

Randy Bacon 56
Mary Baxter 60
David Caton 63
Margie Crisp 66
Keith Davis 70
Fidencio Duran 72
Jon Flaming 73
Charles Ford 74
Pat Gabriel 77
Hunter George 80
Billy Hassell 82
Lee Jamison 85
Robb Kendrick 88
Laura Lewis 89
William Montgomery 92
Noe Perez 96
Jeri Salter 100
Erik Sprohge 103
Debbie Stevens 105
William Young 108

About the Artists 111
Index of Rivers 157

ACKNOWLEDGMENTS

As I sit to write the acknowledgments for this title in the River Books series, which is made possible by the unique partnership of Texas A&M University Press and The Meadows Center for Water and the Environment at Texas State University, I am moved not only by the extraordinary beauty of the volume but also by the collaboration with William Reaves | Sarah Foltz Fine Art, a notable Houston-based art gallery. Bill and Sarah have perhaps done more than anyone to promote the appreciation of the sensational body of Texas regional artists who, as demonstrated on these pages, have brought such delight to so many but have also brought attention to the rich cultural and natural history of our state.

Bill would be the first to join me in declaring emphatically that this book would never have been possible without the very significant contributions of many talented and dedicated people who we are lucky to have in our lives. Bill's colleague and partner, Sarah Foltz, helped in editing, photographing, and coordinating permissions from a host of lenders who have allowed their paintings to be included in the project. Artists Margie Crisp and Bill Montgomery worked together to create the beautiful map of Texas rivers.

We are especially grateful to the leadership of institutions across Texas who have arranged for the work on these pages to be featured in exhibitions sponsored by leading venues around the state. To Howard Taylor and Laura Huckaby of the San Angelo Museum of Art, Joe Hammer of the Lady Bird Johnson Wildflower Center in Austin, and Marise McDermott and Randall Webster of the Witte Museum in San Antonio, we are very grateful.

It would have been impossible to assemble this body of work without the generosity of those who trusted us with their paintings for inclusion in both the book and the exhibitions along with the exceptional group of artists who created them.

Bill and I both owe a great debt of gratitude to the staffs of Texas A&M University Press, including its inestimable leader, Shannon Davies, and her colleagues, Thom Lemmons and Katie Duelm. Here at the Meadows Center, Laura Parchman contributed significantly to research on Texas rivers.

Funding for the book was made possible by one of Texas' most distinguished conservationists and a champion of its waterways, Terry Hershey, who coincidentally founded the very first art gallery in Fort Worth and has been a staunch supporter of River Books since the inception of the series. No person has contributed more to the means and opportunity for me to write through the years than Terry.

Finally, perhaps the most satisfying aspect of this project has been to work with and get to know Bill, with whom I hope to do many more projects in the years ahead. Bill shares with me the excitement of appreciating the intersection of art and the environment and the privilege of sharing that excitement and enthusiasm with others.

Bill and I also have fabulous life partners, Linda Reaves and Nona Sansom, who helped with editing and many other essential tasks, but, more importantly, they have never failed to provide us the love and support that allows us to indulge ourselves on wonderful projects like this one.

—Andrew Sansom, General Editor, River Books

RIVERS AND PEOPLE

Andrew Sansom

I'll always remember the night we camped on a sandbar in Santa Elena Canyon. The sheer 1,500-foot walls on both sides of the river that Americans call the Rio Grande rendered our view of the sky a narrow, winding ribbon of blue far above. At twilight, a peregrine falcon swooped down and snatched a quick-flitting Mexican free-tailed bat right out of the air. After the dinner dishes were washed and put away, the ribbon over our heads deepened to a rich indigo, now spangled with a million stars.

Pleasantly tired, we savored the afternoon's run. The river flowing through the canyon was challenging but presented no serious danger to us in our canoes. In the campfire's glow, we looked ahead with anticipation to the day to come. The strong currents of this great river would take us through the imposing formation known as the Rockslide and ultimately out of Santa Elena and into the scorching sun of the Chihuahuan Desert. As we sat comfortably by our campfire, thinking about tomorrow's float, we never dreamed that the day might come when there would not be enough water in the Rio Grande for such an adventure to be possible.

Rivers have wound their way through the human imagination since at least the dawn of recorded time, and, likely, long before that. Some of our earliest stories involve rivers. In the beginning, according to the Old Testament book of Genesis, four rivers flowed out of the Garden of Eden; two of them—the Tigris and Euphrates—fostered one of the world's earliest great civilizations. Some scholars believe that the seasonal river floods of the Levant form the nucleus of the biblical story of the Deluge. Indeed, most of the world's most influential cultures, from Mesopotamia to Egypt and China, have evolved along the banks of rivers, where water was accessible and ensured that civilization could survive and develop. Perhaps as a result, virtually every genre of literature throughout history employs rivers as metaphors for practically every aspect of human experience. Like human life itself, rivers move and flow through the landscape, through the legends of humanity, and through different nations and cultures, trans-

David Caton, Toward Mule Ears from the Mouth of Santa Elena Canyon

forming and evolving as they make the winding journey from their sources to their final destinations. There is little wonder that rivers have found such a prominent position in human expression through literature, music, and art.

Telling River Stories, Singing River Songs

Samuel Langhorne Clemens, who took as his pen name the navigation term "Mark Twain," knew intimately the mythic pull of rivers. Trained in his youth as a riverboat pilot, he turned to writing and penned some of the most memorable river tales in western literature. Twain's work embodies the deep connection between a great river and society. In *The Adventures of Tom Sawyer*, *Pudd'nhead Wilson*, and *Huckleberry Finn*, he wove stories of race, coming of age, social convention, and identity into the encompassing fabric of the river. At the same time, he gave us a serious treatise on the river in his *Life on the Mississippi*.

Thankfully, Twain is not alone in our river library but is accompanied by the likes of Henry David Thoreau in *A Week on the Concord and Merrimack Rivers*, Ernest Hemingway in his story "Big Two-Hearted River," Norman McLean in "A River Runs through It," and Texan John Graves, whose *Goodbye to a River* laments the passing of the Brazos River of his youth, forever altered by dams.

Others have cried out for our rivers in music. Biedrich Smetana's 1874 tone poem *The Moldau*, named for the major river of the composer's native Moldavia and part of his larger work *My Country*, is an intensely patriotic, symphonic evocation of scenes from life along this great European river. Rivers have also been frequently celebrated in song. In fact, the very first song about Texas in the English language was written about the Brazos. In 1831, when Texas was still part of Mexico, Stephen F. Austin's cousin Mary Austin Holley, inspired by her journey up the river to Austin's Colony, wrote "The Brazos Boat Song." Later in the nineteenth century, after the abolition of slavery, vast prison farms sprouted on the former plantations lining the lower Brazos. The inmates sang of their gritty existence in "Ain't No More Cane on the Brazos," a "work song" from a tradition originating in West Africa. This mournful music helped pass the time while creating a cadence and rhythm to synchronize the grueling labor. Called "work songs" in most of America, these chants were called "river songs" in Texas due to their origins on the sprawling and grim prison plantations along the Brazos and the Trinity.

Cowboys, driving cattle north from Texas to railheads in Kansas and Missouri in the mid- to late 1800s, whiled away time on the trail with tunes like "The Texas River Song." Called "the granddaddy of all Texas river songs" by John Wheat, coordinator of sound archives and music history at the Barker Center for American History at the University of Texas in Austin, "The Texas River Song" mentions no fewer than fourteen Texas rivers. Though more than one hundred years old, it is sung to this day, having been recorded by prominent Texas musicians such as Townes Van Zandt and Lyle Lovett. There have been many other songs about Texas rivers, including "Sleepy Rio Grande" by Gene Autry, "Matamoros Banks" by Bruce Springsteen, "Just Across the Rio Grande" by Reba McEntire, "Rio Grande" by Brian Wilson, and many more.

Mary Baxter, Last Light Near Fresno Canyon

Perhaps the seemingly universal connection between rivers and music is best explained by Kevin Anderson, who directs the Austin Water Center for Environmental Research. In his lecture on culture and rivers, Anderson says, "Rivers sing. There's always music in a river. It's everything from the gurgling sounds to the rapids. If you analyzed the melodies of all the Texas river songs, there's an aspect of the flow of the river in all of them. Songs let us celebrate rivers."

Picturing Rivers

So do paintbrush and canvas. It seems likely that humans have been making pictures about rivers for as long as they have been making music about them. For centuries, artists have created images—on cave walls and on canvas—that have evoked both the physical and metaphysical aspects of rivers. Even Renaissance man Leonardo da Vinci was fascinated by flowing water. Leonardo flourished at the intersection of art and science and studied both as a painter and a hydrological engineer. He described water as "the vehicle of nature," viewing rivers and streams serving our planet as blood serves our bodies. The first to describe the principle of erosion, Leonardo said, "Water gnaws at mountains and fills valleys. If it could, it would reduce the Earth to a perfect sphere." He feared the destructive capacity of water and depicted terrible floods and inundations in his writings and drawings.

Three hundred years later, as noted hereafter by my good friend and collaborator William Reaves, the New World witnessed the emergence of an art movement known as the Hudson River School. The works of this group of mid-nineteenth-century artists romantically portrayed the Hudson River and surrounding area. They also reflected the America of the time in themes of discovery, exploration, and settlement. In a harbinger of present-day Texas, artists of the Hudson River School, including Thomas Cole, Albert Bierstadt, and Thomas Moran, were known for their realistic, detailed, and sometimes idealistic renditions of nature and the wilderness that was disappearing before their eyes as the region developed and urbanized.

I'll leave most of the responsibility for discussing the work of Texas regional artists, as represented in this book, to William; his expertise in Texas art and artists far exceeds mine. I will say, however, that it is deeply gratifying to me, as a lifelong advocate of the conservation and protection of our natural heritage, to see how the work of Texas artists has come to constitute an eloquent plea for the preservation of one of the continent's most beautiful, and yes, romantic landscapes.

Making Art, Saving Rivers

In fact, art in service to the earth is well represented in American tradition. Support for the establishment of the great national parks of the west, including Yosemite and Yellowstone, was greatly influenced by the stunning masterpieces of Moran and Bierstadt. No person is more linked with the protection of birds in America than John James Audubon, whose popular images brought to the nation both the beauty of birds and knowledge of their precarious plight. In the twentieth century, Roger Tory Peterson followed in Audubon's wake, introducing the enjoyment of birdwatching and bird identification to millions through his art and public advocacy.

Likewise, Texas artists have traditionally celebrated the so-called "consumptive" outdoor life. Their images of hunting and fishing have raised millions of dollars for conservation. In fact, the first painting I ever bought was a duck hunting scene. It was hanging in a gallery in Lubbock, located above the bookstore where I acquired my textbooks each semester as a student at Texas Tech University. I would visit the bookstore at the beginning of each term, buy my books, and then head up to the gallery. One year, the owner noticed that I always visited the same painting and asked if I were interested in purchasing it. Though I loved the piece, it was well beyond my means, but he allowed me to leave the painting in the store and pay him around ten dollars a month, which I could afford. I picked it up when I graduated three years later, and it is hanging in my home today.

William Montgomery, Tropical Parulas on Pulliam Creek

Perhaps the reason I was so drawn to this painting was because of the pull of rivers, not only on the human imagination, but also on the cycle of nature itself. Of course, the two frequently intersect. My childhood on the Texas coast, for example, was indelibly marked by the spectacle of millions of migratory waterfowl returning each year for the winter. I knew my birthday was coming when, in October each year, I began to hear the cries of migrating geese overhead in the night. My friends and I spent as much time as possible in the marshes, hunting and fishing in these places where fresh water from the rivers mingles with salt water from the sea. These are still among my most treasured pastimes and memories today, and I still listen for the haunting call of the geese in October. The wintering habitat for these wonderful birds is largely created by that mix of fresh and salt water that results in a brackish environment that supplies vital food and shelter for these first winter Texans—all made possible by the intersection of river and ocean.

Water Fights

And yet, there are still those in Texas—some of our leaders among them—who believe that the last drop of water going over the last dam and into the Gulf of Mexico is water wasted. It is a grim reality that in Texas, as elsewhere in the world, the contest over the uses to which water should be put—and who has the right to decide on those uses—is intense and escalating. This is made even more worrisome by the fact, as documented by water rights expert Charles R. Porter in his book *Sharing the Common Pool: Water Rights in the Everyday Lives of Texans*, that if all the legal rights to water in Texas were fully asserted, there would not be

Hunter George, Crossing the Guadalupe

enough water—in the rivers, underground, or anywhere else—to fully satisfy the demand. Add to this the expectation that our population here in the Lone Star State will double by mid-century, and we arrive at the frightening realization that we have already given permission for more water to be withdrawn from many of our rivers than is actually in them.

To put it bluntly: if all of the water rights issued in Texas since we were a colony of Spain were fully exercised, many of our most iconic rivers would be dry today. In fact, at the end of the twentieth century, we saw a chilling foreshadowing of such a condition when, for a time, the once-mighty Rio Grande no longer reached its mouth on the Gulf of Mexico. And as the population of our state continues to grow, we are almost guaranteed to strain our rivers as never before and then increase pumping of groundwater, thus threatening the springs that nourish many of our most picturesque rivers and streams, particularly those of the Texas Hill Country.

As a child, my favorite river was the Guadalupe. Each summer our family would head inland from the Coast to the upper reaches of the "Guad," where relatives had a camp on the South Fork above Kerrville. Where we lived, in the southeastern part of the state, the rivers were murky and slow-moving, so the crystal-clear, swift, cool waters of the upper Guadalupe were magical to us. We swam and skipped rocks in the river, learned the skills and joys of canoeing through its rapids, and fell asleep to its murmuring at night.

In the years that followed, I ran the demanding but spectacular Devils River, the Frio, the Nueces, the Llano, the Lampasas, and other Hill Country watercourses. The primary point of access to the Devils River for paddlers like me is at Baker's Crossing, a tiny hamlet where State Highway 163 crosses the river. The Devils, created by spring flow out of the far west side of the Edwards Plateau, is undoubtedly the most unspoiled stream in Texas. Its pristine nature is largely due to the fact that most of its banks have traditionally been owned by fiercely private landowners for whom downriver paddling is basically considered a nuisance.

If you are hardy enough to run it, though, both the challenges and rewards are substantial. As you glide downstream and leave behind what little civilization exists at Baker's Crossing, the flow and extraordinary purity of the river increase as even larger springs continuously augment the current. Alternating between crystalline pools and often difficult rapids, the run downstream of about twenty-five miles to Dolan Falls, the largest waterfall in Texas, is an odyssey of both ecstasy and ordeal.

Now largely protected by the Nature Conservancy of Texas and the Texas Parks and Wildlife Department, the Devils River corridor consists of a rich blend of spectacular topography, vegetation, and wildlife. Situated at the confluence of the Edwards Plateau, the Chihuahuan Desert, and the Tamaulipan Plain, the river traverses one of the richest troves of biodiversity in Texas.

It is very dry here. Throughout human occupation of the region, the inhabitants have, out of necessity, been tough, but the original people of the Devils River were also intensely cultured, as evidenced by the deeply spiritual rock art still visible on cave walls along the river.

I have many memories of exploring those river caves, especially one occupied by a more recent but equally rugged cave dweller. Though there is ample evidence of human activity along the river—including a crossing used by the first Spanish explorer of Texas, Cabeza de Vaca; traces of the Comacheria; and more—the first permanent settlement since the time of the indigenous people was in this cave. A really tough eighteen-year-old from Gonzales County, H. K. Fawcett, came out to the Devils River on horseback to help drive the last spikes in the transcontinental railroad on the Union Pacific tracks near the Pecos River, close by. Fawcett's diary was written on the walls of the cave and may still be seen there today.

From this humble beginning on the banks of the Devils River, he helped found the most expansive wool industry in America. Though the millions of sheep in this empire were undoubtedly hard on the land, by the mid-twentieth century, Fawcett owned more than 100,000 acres and had become one of the most respected and influential citizens of the region, assisting Amon Carter in establishing the Big Bend National Park. Today, his once-vast domain has become the basis for extensive public and private land conservation in the river basin. I remember thinking of H. K. Fawcett and his little cave at the legal ceremony that established the Devils River State Natural Area, which came about when extensive debt caused Fawcett's great realm to slip from the hands of his heirs. I know, however, that he would be pleased that the magnificent legacy he assembled along this beautiful river is still visible for the enrichment of all Texans. Each year his descendants still gather at the cave where it all began.

David Caton, Botkin Ranch

Water Is Life

Though there is much richness and beauty in both the landscape and culture of the Hill Country, it is the springs and the watercourses in this region at the very heart of Texas that draw us there in greater numbers than in any other region of the United States. As a result, our Hill Country springs are threatened as never before. Fueling this ominous circumstance is the fact that, as our rivers are largely over committed, we are increasingly dependent on water from our aquifers to meet the needs of Texas' exploding population.

This shift did not occur overnight. San Antonio, for example, relies exclusively on the Edwards Aquifer for essentially all of its municipal and industrial use, largely because Texas historically has avoided any regulation of groundwater pumping. Today, thankfully, pumping from the Edwards Aquifer is controlled, but only because the huge springs at San Marcos and New Braunfels, home to several endangered or threatened species, were threatened by reduced flow.

A digression: I go to work each day in what was known for many years as the Aquarena Springs Inn on the shores of Spring Lake, the headwaters of the San Marcos River, which flows into the Guadalupe. Spring Lake is formed by the San Marcos Springs, the second largest artesian spring in the western United States, and an ancient dam built by Edward Burleson, the first vice president of the Republic of Texas. The crystal-clear water and the karst system from which it emerges are home to eight federally listed endangered and threatened species, and the lake bottom houses the remains of possibly the oldest continuously inhabited site in North America. My office is in the honeymoon suite of the old hotel, which was restored largely with funding from the Texas Parks and Wildlife Department. In exchange for that funding, my employer, Texas State University, quietly conveyed 40,000 acre-feet of its water rights to environmental flows that will stay in the river forever. It is the largest commitment of water to environmental flows ever made in Texas.

Unfortunately, this level of generosity is not often practiced elsewhere in Texas, and the courts continue to rule that groundwater is the property of the surface owner. In this regard, I always think of the Blanco, which springs from the earth out in Kendall County, south of Fredericksburg. The river flows southeastward toward Hays County where I work, and before it reaches the county line, most of its flow sinks back into the ground through the riverbed. From there, the river flows underground to a lovely Hill Country spring called Jacob's Well, where it reemerges from the earth, flows down Cypress Creek through the city of Wimberley, and ultimately goes back into the Blanco. If you tried to get a water rights permit to take any appreciable amount of water out of the Blanco, it would, in all likelihood, be denied, because most if not all of the surface water in the river is already committed. If, however, you drilled a well into the underground river above Jacob's Well, you could pretty much pump as much groundwater as you like with little regulation and few permit requirements.

Historically, the surface water in our rivers and streams is considered by law to be public property while water underground is private property. The Texas legislature enabled the creation of groundwater conservation districts in Texas toward the end of the twentieth century to try to manage water use. However, virtually all wells for residential, agricultural, or oil and gas use are exempted from regulation. Further, many of the nearly one hundred districts that have been created are organized by county lines rather than aquifers, are underfunded, and have little science to guide their decisions. Finally, the courts have continued to rule in favor of landowners' rights to the water under their land. It is no wonder that various investment groups and entrepreneurs in the Panhandle, Trans-Pecos, and Central Texas are scrambling to pump millions of gallons of groundwater and sell it to thirsty cities without any particular concern for the consequences. We have little choice but to increasingly look to groundwater to quench the thirst of our growing population, but refusing to link it in law and regulation to surface water—to continue to pretend that, despite the hydrological connection of the two, one belongs to the public and the other is private property—is potentially catastrophic, especially for the rivers and streams of the Hill Country. This hydrologically illogical circumstance is sure to bring many disputes in the years to come as landowners who wish to pump water from the aquifers are pitted against water rights holders downstream along the rivers of Texas who have been told that water from the same source belongs to them.

My wife and I returned to the old family camp on the spring-fed

Keith Davis, Tubing Down the Guadalupe

Guadalupe for our honeymoon, and I desperately hope that our grandchildren will be able, as we did, to skip rocks and swim in its clear, cooling waters. Time will tell. Unfortunately, dealing with these kinds of problems in our legislature has been possible only when politicians are faced with a federal court order or a natural disaster.

Drought and Flood

Such a disaster occurred in the early 1950s in the form of a drought that we have traditionally called "the drought of record," which might be translated to "as bad as it is going to get." In those days, most Texans lived on farms and ranches or in small towns dependent upon agriculture. When the drought came, it was up close and personal. In the best book written about drought to date—*The Time It Never Rained*, by West Texas native Elmer Kelton—the story of rancher Charlie Floyd is almost too painful to read. Indeed, many who grew up in the era refuse to do so; their memories of the drought are just that harrowing.

The drought in those days was bad at Stonewall in the Hill Country, where I write today, very near the Pedernales River, which, in September 1952 had ceased to flow, reflecting how indifferent rivers are to our needs. They are sometimes bountiful, sometimes dry…and sometimes violent.

Such was the case on September 9 of that year, in the depths of the drought, when twenty-six inches of rain fell on Stonewall and the surrounding countryside in a matter of hours. For the previous week, the Pedernales, which borders the LBJ Ranch, had no flow whatsoever. But by September 11, the river was forty-two feet above normal, isolating the children at the Stonewall school for three days, sweeping an eighteen-wheeler carrying nineteen tons of structural steel off the highway and four hundred yards downstream, and obliterating the bridge over Highway 281 above Johnson City.

At that time, due to the sustained drought, Lake Travis, fed primarily by the Pedernales, was at an all-time low, less than one-third its normal level. As the raging floodwaters surged toward the lake on September 11, the Pedernales was fully sixty feet above normal. At the low-water crossing on Hamilton Pool Road near the town of Bee Cave, it flowed at an astonishing volume, greater than that of the Mississippi River, and it increased the level of Lake Travis by fifty-seven feet between 1:00 a.m. and noon. For the first time since the drought began, the lake was full. But the drought went on for five more years.

More recently, my Labrador retriever, Scout, and I walked with friends along the Blanco River in Hays County on a wonderful late-winter quail hunt. The Blanco emerges from Hill Country springs in Kendall County, south of Fredericksburg, and flows some eighty-seven miles to our hunting site that day between Wimberley and San Marcos. Just south of there, its pale green waters join the San Marcos River, which then joins the Guadalupe at Luling and rolls on down to San Antonio Bay on the Gulf of Mexico.

Erik Sprohge, River Rock

That day, the birds were flying well and the scenting conditions were perfect for the pointing dogs; Scout was having the time of her life retrieving birds shot over the river. On past hunts, the shooting was made challenging by the huge cypress trees, hundreds of years old, lining the banks and giving the wily quail some cover on the wing. But this time, the trees were gone.

On May 24, 2015, approximately ten inches of rain fell in the Blanco River basin onto a landscape already saturated from above-normal rainfall. The river rose some forty feet above normal at Wimberley and roared downstream, killing thirteen people and demolishing or seriously damaging hundreds of homes and thousands of majestic trees—including the centuries-old cypresses lining the river.

To this date, two children who were lost in the flood have never been found, and the loss of the magnificent trees will change the character of the river corridor for hundreds of years. The Guadalupe–Blanco River Authority, steward of the water in these rivers, conducted a study in 2011 using tree ring samples from the big trees to determine historic patterns of drought. One of the trees in the study was determined to have emerged on the river back in 1426, nearly a century before the Spanish explorers first arrived in Texas. The river is still beautiful, but it has been profoundly changed by the loss of the great sentinels along its banks that had seen many cycles of flooding and drought through their long lifetimes.

Changing Rivers in a Changing Texas

After the drought of the 1950s, Texas embarked on an unprecedented drive to make sure such huge economic and social losses never happened again. Our current water planning process and much of the water infrastructure on which we depend—especially the many dams that were constructed to form lakes that still provide water for hundreds of Texas communities—came out of the "drought of record." Though that infrastructure helped get us to the twenty-first century and underpinned unparalleled economic prosperity, our wild rivers were forever altered. Further, most of us have moved into town, making Texas one of America's most urban states.

Texas' shift from a rural, bucolic society to an almost totally urban one has produced many transformational effects. Most children in Texas now grow to adulthood without ever experiencing or even comprehending the beauty of the rural countryside or the contributions that city dwellers receive from the landscape and the rivers and streams that nourish it. Unfortunately, as political and economic power has shifted to urban Texas, concern for the lands and waters of rural Texas diminishes, and as the rush for water accelerates, the health of our natural springs and watercourses becomes an increasingly low and little-understood priority. Additionally, the fact that most rivers in Texas are bounded primarily by privately owned land further limits the urban dweller from knowing or appreciating them.

Another unfortunate aspect of that limitation is the resulting misconception that the deterioration of the landscape in Texas is the result of modernity and industrialization. As renowned naturalist David Schmidly portrayed in his seminal work *Texas Natural History: A Century of Change*, the landscape of our state is actually in much better condition than it was in the late nineteenth century when all of the timber in East Texas had been cut and much of the rest of the state was so overgrazed that the Texas Hill Country, for example, lost fifteen inches of soil. It was, at that time, along with Appalachia, one of the poorest regions in the United States. Today, through the efforts of more educated landowners and the assistance of the Texas Soil and Water Conservation Board, Texas' Soil and Water Conservation Districts, the Natural Resource Conservation

Service, and the Texas Parks and Wildlife Department, the landscape of Texas and its river banks, recharge areas, and watersheds are in pretty good shape. Thanks to improved stewardship, the health of the countryside contributes directly to our rivers and streams, as erosion is contained, watershed function is strengthened, and absorption of rainfall into the soil and the aquifers is enhanced.

Nevertheless, despite a century of success on the landscape, the watersheds, recharge areas, and riparian zones that sustain our rivers and streams in Texas are faced with an even more ominous threat: the increased fragmentation of rural lands. Here at Stonewall on the historic Hershey Ranch, a pipeline was laid in 1928 to carry crude oil to refineries along the coast. At that time, in order to cross Gillespie County, where the ranch is located, the pipeline company had to deal with only twelve landowners. In 2011, the pipeline was removed, and the company, along the same route, had to negotiate with 2,000 separate landowners.

The accelerating breakup of ancestral lands in Texas places our rivers and streams in jeopardy as never before. As a result of our entry into the United States as an independent nation, Texas retained ownership of its public lands and promptly sold them off to finance the Capitol, the government, and our schools. Thus, more than ninety-five percent of the landscape of the Lone Star State is now privately owned and, though generally well-managed, is breaking up before our eyes: increasing pollution, impeding recharge, and altering the rainwater catchment function of our watersheds. In addition, most of the resulting smaller tracts of land from this vast breakup contain wells dug by the new owners; this adds exponentially to the strain on our groundwater—and, following the flow, on our rivers.

We lost more than a million acres of farmland and ranchland in the decade between 1997 and 2007. Largely due to a lack of understanding by our urban population of the benefits we receive from the countryside, we have done almost nothing to stem the tide.

This lack of understanding, along with the shift of economic and political power to the cities, has accelerated the disturbing lack of consideration for rural areas and small towns. Today, the great cities of North and Central Texas along Interstate 35 campaign for reservoirs on undisturbed stretches of East Texas rivers, including the Neches and Sulphur,

William Montgomery, Fish Story I

Keith Davis, Fishing on Town Lake at Sunset with Bats

and seek to extract massive amounts of groundwater from aquifers east of the urban sprawl, threatening the flows of rivers like the Colorado and the Brazos.

While it is a fact that water is plentiful in East Texas, it is also true that some of our most precious aquatic resources, which are dependent on that water, are located there as well. Much of the concern over proposed construction of additional reservoirs on rivers in East Texas originated from the threat such infrastructure poses on low-lying areas of the Piney Woods that are periodically or permanently inundated. These flooded river bottoms along the Neches, the Sulphur, the Sabine, and the Angelina are home to some of the most significant stands of hardwood timber in the South.

Nowhere is this importance more exemplified and revealed than at Caddo Lake, recognized by the United Nations as a wetland of international significance. Formed by a vast, ancient logjam in the Red River that backed up its tributary Cypress Bayou, Caddo Lake became what most believe to be the only natural lake in Texas. In the first of many water control actions in East Texas, the US Army Corps of Engineers removed the logjam in 1874 to facilitate navigation to Shreveport and very nearly destroyed Caddo Lake forever.

The tradition of massive water projects, which began with the removal of the Red River logjam and included the building of many reservoirs in the region, has obliterated many of the flooded river bottoms that have been called the "rainforests of Texas." These river and stream bottoms shelter all that is left of one of the most diverse biological resources in Texas. In our rush to store and move water westward, care must be taken, lest in the process we destroy a rich and unique regional culture and one of the most beautiful places on the earth.

Actually, virtually all of Texas' vast network of rivers and streams has been altered in some way; there are very few virgin streams left in our state. In many ways, the massive alteration has served us well, enabling our rivers to become lovely amenities in cities. Each year, thousands of city dwellers enjoy Lady Bird Lake in Austin, the Riverwalk in San Antonio, Buffalo Bayou in Houston, and the Trinity River as it flows through the Dallas–Fort Worth Metroplex.

I once canoed the Trinity through Irving near Texas Stadium. The contrast between the gleaming metropolitan development and the quiet flow of the river's Elm Fork was remarkable as we left the former behind and entered a world unknown to most of its nearby human inhabitants. The great American landscape architect Frederick Law Olmstead, designer of Central Park in New York City, visited Texas in the nineteenth century and described this reach of the Trinity as having an "almost tropical aspect." Olmstead wrote of immense trees with interlocking branches, massive grapevines, and luxuriant Spanish moss. Thankfully, the remains of this primeval forest are with us today, south of downtown Dallas, along the river's muddy meanders.

Randy Bacon, The Bridges at Samuels Avenue

Interestingly, Olmstead also described the Trinity more than 150 years ago as "the most navigable stream in Texas." He wasn't the only one. Through the years there have been numerous efforts to bring commercial navigation to the Metroplex, as it is the only major metropolitan area in the United States not served by a major waterway or port. As the population has exploded, however, the river has been mainly viewed as a source of water to fuel this growth—both in the Dallas–Fort Worth area and in Houston—and as a conduit to carry away the effluent of urbanity.

In the years ahead, the fights will not likely be over navigation but will probably stem from the fact that nearly every drop of water from the Trinity, consumed by the citizens of Houston located at the river's mouth, has already been through the wastewater treatment plants of Dallas and Fort Worth. As pressure to provide more water for the municipal growth upstream intensifies, increasing efforts will be made to "reuse" treated wastewater, potentially reducing the flow of the river and, in turn, threatening the welfare of those who live, work, and play downstream. For now, happily, the Trinity has been rediscovered and promises to join other urban rivers in Texas that are increasingly understood as contributions to the quality of life in the city, blending infrastructure for flood control, aesthetics, and opportunities for recreation.

The many dams built in Texas after the drought of the 1950s have shielded us from the devastation of drought and flood, brought recreation to millions, and produced perhaps the finest bass fishing in America. The massive water infrastructure that includes nearly 200 major reservoirs helped fuel the miraculous growth that has made Texas the second largest economy in the country and the twelfth largest in the world.

Fidencio Duran, The Crossing

Still, there is no question that providing sufficient water in the new century for the fastest-growing region in the United States is our foremost dilemma. The tragedy is that our attempts to quench our growing thirst threaten some of our most significant waterways, yet we continue to consume water as if our supply were infinite.

Rivers connect us. The Rio Grande/Río Bravo ties the Rocky Mountains in Colorado to the Chihuahuan Desert in Texas and Mexico and ultimately to the Gulf of Mexico. Rivers provide a conjunction of diverse ecosystems and a continuum through past and present, connecting us with our history. And yet, rivers can also separate us, dividing one nation from another, splitting communities, and even isolating families. Indeed, rivers flow through a landscape of rich contradictions, all of which, individually or together, provide us with both tangible evidence of the physical impact they have on our lives and also with windows through which we can find meaning.

Cherishing Texas Rivers

My love of the beauty of nature, I am sure, springs from my childhood on the banks of Oyster Creek, just inside the great hardwood forest along the Texas coastal plain. My grandmother taught me how to fish, a pastime that continues to enrich my life today; I fished in the creek behind my house every chance I got.

My father was not an outdoorsman, but I am eternally grateful that he recognized that the outdoors was a passion of mine and that he did everything he could to nourish it. Knowing how much I loved the creek, he helped me build a wooden boat in our garage. When finished, it opened up a whole new world for me. Every day, returning from school, I would launch my boat and explore the creek, experiencing the mystery and adventure of not always knowing what lay around the next bend. I learned that my disposition changed with every stroke of the oars as I fell into the rhythm of the stream and left the world behind.

I grew to cherish the feeling of being in the wilderness as the dense woodland on the banks of the creek camouflaged the civilization beyond. Huge live oaks grew out over the murky water, creating a tunnel of shade and dappled sunlight and burning a lasting image on my soul.

Many years later I returned to spread my father's ashes on the creek bank where we had spent so much time together. The deep woods along the shore have since yielded to a subdivision, and local authorities have cleared most of the overhanging trees in the name of flood control. My watery tunnel is gone; the creek of my childhood has been altered forever.

My boyhood haunt on Oyster Creek lies near the mouth of another iconic Texas river that the Spanish explorers called *Brazos de Dios*, "Arms of God." In stark contrast to the stars over Santa Elena Canyon, the nightly firmament over the lower Brazos of my childhood was created by the spectacular constellation of lights from the Dow Chemical plants along what is known as the "old river."

The old river is so named because it is the original mouth of the Brazos. Back in the early twentieth century, the river was diverted at Velasco, where Santa Anna was held captive after the battle of San Jacinto. The diversion of the river was meant to ensure that the enormous sediment load the river carried to the Gulf of Mexico each year would flow directly into the sea and away from the harbor at Freeport. One hundred years earlier, the *Lively*, carrying Stephen F. Austin's first boatload of colonists, mistook the Brazos for its intended destination at the mouth of the Colorado and wrecked at the place now known as Quintana. Located where the old river meets the Gulf, Quintana is the oldest Anglo settlement in Texas.

Today, in a rich but discordant tableau of history, natural beauty, and industrialization, you can walk along the beach at Quintana and see artifacts, including bits of china and pottery from Austin's colony, occasionally wash up at your feet against the backdrop of the largest petrochemical complex in the world. This haunting contrast is equally compelling along the San Jacinto River just a few miles away from Quintana, where the toxic emissions of the refineries on the Houston Ship Channel corrode the limestone of the San Jacinto Monument, the principal memorial of Texas' independence from Mexico.

Given the profound importance of rivers to humanity, it is all the more striking that, while we have relied upon our rivers for so many economical, ecological, and spiritual purposes, we have done little to ensure that water will remain in them for fish and other aquatic creatures, for beauty and serenity, and for recreation and the environment. Most of us

Lee Jamison, The Light of Industry, Freeport

Noe Perez, River Road View

have heard the simple and true phrase "water is life"; however, we continue, all too often, to ignore its implications.

I returned to Santa Elena Canyon a while back, and there was so little water flowing that we had to put in at the mouth, which is normally the end of the trip, and paddle upstream to the Rockslide in the still pool of water that is all that remains of the river there. The canyon is still magnificent, and though we were again humbled to be back beneath the lovely ribbon of sky, the flowing Rio Grande is gone, and somehow the great canyon has lost its soul.

As you enjoy the scenes along Texas rivers lovingly rendered by the artists featured in this book, remember how our love of rivers reflects our fundamental need for our rivers to remain healthy and flowing strong. Let these images inspire you to go out and find your own way of enjoying the rivers of Texas. And, as you enjoy them, make up your mind to do what you can to help ensure that future generations of Texans will be able to enjoy them, too.

TRACING THE RIVER AS MUSE IN THE LONE STAR LANDSCAPE

William E. Reaves

I grew up on the rural Texas coast, roaming adjacent gulf prairies and wooded bottom lands around our home situated close to the mouths of three grand rivers. My excursions there fostered an early appreciation of the historical bond that exists between the lives, livelihoods, and lands that surround these great water sources. Every great ranch and farm in our area was sourced in some manner by these rivers or by the sprawling web of tributaries that flowed into them. The gargantuan petrochemical plants that abounded in that country and provided employment for my father fed off of these rivers' resources as well. The small towns and archaic settlements scattered across our county were nestled beside these old rivers, still clinging to them in one way or another for character, recreation, and sustenance. The bountiful rivers that I knew growing up—the Brazos, San Bernard, and Colorado—and the people and wildlife living on them remain as vivid recollections in my mind's eye and have quietly contributed to long-held personal views on matters of nature and life.

Streams of Influence: Encountering the River in Art and Life

Much later, as I began to explore art, it dawned on me that those same youthful exploits across the coastal plains must have also sowed within me a natural affinity for the painted image of the Texas landscape—especially a fondness for landscapes with rivers running through them. As I grew to appreciate landscape painting as one of the powerful and elegant modes of artistic expression, I began to recognize yet another important attribute of the rivers in our midst—as essential creative forces that have inspired and shaped the course of our art and artists throughout history. Having now viewed many American landscape paintings in a career of collecting and dealing in art, it is apparent to me that our finest artists, both past and present, have been as profoundly moved by the rivers that they have encountered in their lives as I have been by the rivers encountered in my own.

In fact, the first great school of American art was inspired by a river. In the United States of the 1830s, American painter Thomas Cole (1801–1848) and a pioneering band of artists on the Eastern seaboard were already at work producing romantic landscape paintings celebrating the verdant scenes of a new nation. Bolstered by American economic prosperity and the emergent patron class of a rapidly growing populous, this first wave of American artists capitalized on a buoyant national identity and excitement for all things natural to forge the first distinctly American "school" of painting—the Hudson River School. Over the following fifty years, American landscapes found growing favor among critics, collectors, and literati of the day, and they continue today to be one of the country's most enduring and popular art forms.[1]

It is not coincidental that this first American school of art carries the moniker of a great river, for it was the course of the Hudson River that directly or indirectly supplied the bulk of source material for these pioneering painters, and for many of these earliest painters it was the river that supplied the necessary modes of transportation to propel them cross-county to such inspiring locales in the first place. While not all Hudson River paintings literally portrayed the river's ebbs and flows in their respective compositions, all of the Hudson River painters rendered devoted interpretations of the grandeur of the land and life that was ultimately shaped and sustained by the coursing waters of the Hudson. Later, as the American landscape expanded further west, these Hudson River painters also expanded their geographical boundaries, traveling ever further to the edges of the new American frontier to paint fantastical landscapes inspired by other prominent rivers and water sources of the vast national expanse. Thus the character of a river gave rise to the most classic genre of American art.

Springs of Creativity: The Texas River Painting Tradition

In the case of our own state, it has been said that all great Texas art is landscape inspired. If this is true, then Texas rivers must surely hold a place of prominence as the seminal inspiration of that landscape. Perhaps more than any other element of the natural environment, the rivers of our state have provided a backdrop for painters in their quests to convey the beauty and grandeur of Texas. How could it be any other way, really? Texas holds 15 major rivers and some 3,700 streams and stretches over 3,300 miles of tidal shoreline.[2] Our river system gives form to Texas and forges the very shape of the Lone Star State. Rivers trace the limits of our towns and the bounds of our counties and lend character and countenance to our bold and distinctive landscape. They nourish the flora and fauna that define and sustain us. Our most storied landforms are chiseled and molded by rivers that have coursed through them for eons, and it would be impossible for artists to convey the geographic definitions of the Lone Star State without their reliance on the vital trails of rivers that string through the hills, plains, and canyons of our state. It is, therefore, only natural that Texas rivers and the myriad life forms concentrated around them have beckoned to Texas artists from the very outset.

In fact, the new Republic of Texas was barely underway when Navy Secretary Samuel Rhoads Fisher and President Sam Houston received America's renowned artist and ornithologist John James Audubon (1785–1851) as a special guest of state. He arrived in Galveston in late April of 1837, and it was Audubon's research that drew him to Texas to observe and paint the rich and abundant bird life that thrived along the rivers, bayous, and estuaries of the lower Texas coast. Detained briefly on Galveston Island, Audubon recorded shore birds on the island's beaches and inlets, painting native species of terns and sandpipers and recording the glorious roseate spoonbill. Despite spring flooding, the artist proceeded to the mouth of the Trinity River to observe avian life on its dank and swampy banks, and he eventually churned up Buffalo Bayou to the newly established capital of Houston, where he found crowds of Texians (including President Houston) still groggy from celebrating their first anniversary of freedom from Mexico. Despite the primitive state of the young Republic and its lack of cultural amenities, Audubon took special note of the wealth of bird life and other wildlife in the fledgling country, and the notes and specimens garnered from his Texas river excursions contributed significantly to the eventual publication of his mammoth portfolio, *Birds of America*.[3]

The late 1840s saw the rise of German immigration into the new state

Karl Hermann Lungkwitz, Above the Fall on the Pedernales River, *1883, oil on canvas, 19 x 27 inches. The Bobbie and John L. Nau Collection of Texas Art*

Pedernales River

of Texas and the first wave of formally trained landscape artists to permanently settle within the Lone Star State. Coming through ports of Galveston and Indianola, they moved inland along the course of Texas rivers such as the Colorado, Guadalupe, and Pedernales, eventually populating the northernmost frontiers of the upper Hill Country.

Prominent among these early German artists were Hermann Lungkwitz (1813–1891) and Richard Petri (1824–1857), two brothers-in-law who had trained together at the Royal Academy of Fine Arts in Dresden and eventually moved, along with their extended families, to the tiny village of Fredericksburg in 1852.[4] While both artist-settlers religiously worked the land in efforts to prove themselves as farmers, they also sketched and painted their new-found country, often sending works back to their native country to acquaint family and friends with their new surroundings. True to their orientation toward German Romanticism, Lungkwitz and Petri often recorded the rivers and creeks adjacent to the Lungkwitz properties in their drawings and paintings of the period. Of the pair, Lungkwitz was the most prolific in his landscape output, his paintings essentially serving as precursors for an eventual school of Hill Country painters who would become paramount in the opening decades of the twentieth century. Lungkwitz was at his best when painting the flowing rivers cutting through the Edwards Plateau, and in works such as *Above the Fall on the Pedernales River*, he aptly captures the romantic aura and appeal of the region's rock-ribbed streams. Had he lived longer, Petri would have no doubt contributed important river imagery to the Texas legacy as well, but regrettably it was the river itself that led to his own demise. In a tragic loss to the state's early art fortunes, Petri, sick and in a fevered delirium, drowned in the Pedernales only five years after his relocation to the state.

By the close of the nineteenth century, images of Texas rivers had found their way into the compositions of Robert Onderdonk (1852–1917) and Frank Reaugh (1860–1945), the two men who had by then emerged as the state's most prominent landscape painters and art instructors. Robert Onderdonk was especially fond of urban river subjects common in his hometown of San Antonio and its environs. As such, he was among the first to convey the river as an essential centerpiece of urban life, painting the San Antonio River with the associated mills, homesteads, and commercial structures that cropped up along its banks as the city grew.[5] Reaugh, on the other hand, was a devotee of the open range and the Texas cattle play, and along with his prominent students, he often sketched on the banks of rivers and streams that crossed the prairies of North and

Frank Reaugh, A Watering Place, Brazos River, *ca. 1900, pastel, 3.5 x 7 inches. Collection of Panhandle-Plains Historical Museum, Canyon*

Brazos River

Robert Jenkins Onderdonk, Falls at Guenther's Lower Mill, *1880, oil on canvas, 14 x 10 inches. The Bobbie and John L. Nau Collection of Texas Art*

San Antonio River

West Texas. In numerous field studies and exquisite studio landscapes, Reaugh painted many Texas rivers, including the Brazos, portraying them as he encountered them, most often as adjuncts to the land that embraced them and the cattle that lived on it.

The popular interest in Texas landscape painting and the allure of river subject matter continued throughout the start of the twentieth century as the state's cultural resources blossomed. Julian Onderdonk (1882–1927), who rose to greatness as a heralded "bluebonnet painter," also painted Texas rivers. In 1912, Onderdonk, only back in Texas for three years from formal training in New York under William Merritt Chase (1849–1916), accepted a commission from the Martindale family to paint their ranch home alongside a favored swimming hole on the San Marcos River. In a large and beautiful oil painting, gripping in both its color and flow, Onderdonk rendered the site in late afternoon sunlight, accentuating the aquamarine tones of the waters flowing fast over a concrete spillway that still exists today. He returned to the subject of Texas rivers on several occasions

Julian Onderdonk, Late Afternoon on the San Marcos River at Martindale, Texas, *1912, oil on canvas, 30 x 40 inches. Collection of Beth and David Dike*

San Marcos River

during the following decade, but, regrettably, his output was cut short by an untimely death at the age of 40 in 1922.

Despite the loss of Onderdonk, the 1920s became an otherwise explosive and productive period for the visual arts in Texas. Supported by newly founded art leagues and art museums in the state's major cities, which offered significant new exhibition venues, the extraordinary work of many more Texas artists came to the fore. Impressionist landscapes continued to hold sway as the dominant genre of the day, and these works frequently addressed the natural beauty of Texas rivers. Among the San Antonio painters who assumed the mantel of landscape painting were José Arpa (1858–1952), Rolla Taylor (1871–1970), and Peter Hohnstedt (1871–1957), all of whom participated in and won awards in the storied Davis Competitions of the late 1920s, and all of whom were known to incorporate river subject matter in their work, appreciating the values and force of water in their landscape compositions. Arpa's *Headwaters of San Antonio* is a direct, early afternoon scene featuring

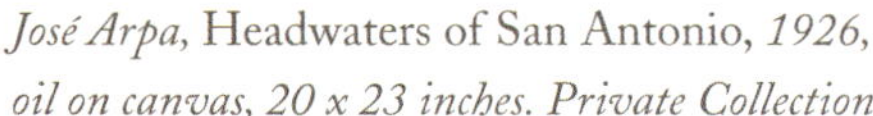

José Arpa, Headwaters of San Antonio, *1926, oil on canvas, 20 x 23 inches. Private Collection*

San Antonio River

Rolla Taylor, The Winding River (San Antonio River), *ca. 1930, oil on canvas board, 20 x 16 inches. Collection of Mr. Robert P. Cochran*

San Antonio River

the play of sunlight on the source waters of the San Antonio River just before it begins meandering through Brackenridge Park. It is illustrative of the artist's ongoing deference to pure landscape paintings and the strong elements of light, shadow, and atmosphere employed in his paintings.

Much in the style of Robert Onderdonk, Rolla Taylor seemed to prefer the distinctive architectural landscape of the San Antonio River, frequently painting the houses and business structures that lined the river's banks. A splendid example is Taylor's 1930s-era painting *Winding River*, featuring the home on the San Antonio River's meandering path through the city. In developing his compositions, such as *Texas Hills*, ca. 1932, Peter Hohnstedt expertly employed the river as an aid to enhance the depth and perspective of classic Hill Country landscapes. By faintly threading the Guadalupe River far below in grand panoramic view, he masterfully guides the eye onward into the heart of the painting through a broad, rolling river valley that ultimately rises to massive cloud banks on the far side.

The San Antonio impressionists, however, were not alone in their affinity for Texas rivers. Farther down state, amid the river bottoms and

Peter L. Hohnstedt, Texas Hills, *ca. 1932, oil on canvas, 25 x 29 inches. Collection of Linda and Bill Reaves*

Guadalupe River

bayou country surrounding Houston, a coterie of female artists took up river subject matter as well. Led by local luminaries such as Emma Richardson Cherry (1858–1954), Grace Spaulding John (1890–1972), and Ruth Pershing Uhler (1895–1967), a small colony of primarily female painters formed and began to exhibit their wares cooperatively. Like Audubon before them, these women soon discovered the splendid landscape and wildlife material afforded by the abundant rivers and streams stretching across the coastal plains surrounding Houston. The group frequently organized painting day trips, sketching on site and exploring the exotic waterways in the vicinities around them. Fortunately, grand examples of these "water works" exist today. In *Smoke, Steam, and Mist #2 (Allen's Landing)*, Grace Spaulding John captured the bustle and brimming atmosphere of Houston's early port commerce, which was concentrated on the shores of Buffalo Bayou and at the foot of Main Street.

Emma Cherry also captured the essence of Buffalo Bayou in her incredible 1937 painting titled *Flood Control on Buffalo Bayou*, which offers testament to the waterway's significance as a centerpiece in the

Grace Spaulding John, Smoke, Steam, and Mist #2 (Allen's Landing), *1924, oil on canvas, 20.13 x 18.13 inches. Courtesy of The Bryan Museum, Galveston*

Buffalo Bayou

Emma Richardson Cherry, Flood Control on Buffalo Bayou, *1937, oil on canvas, 30 x 40 inches. The Bobbie and John L. Nau Collection of Texas Art*

Buffalo Bayou

Ruth Pershing Uhler, Decoration: Red Haw Trees, *1932, oil on canvas, 40 x 52 inches. The Bobbie and John L. Nau Collection of Texas Art*

Buffalo Bayou

city's growth and development, then, as it is now. Ruth Uhler, one of the city's early "modernist" painters, also concerned herself with local rivers and bayous as subjects of her work, albeit with a more modernist style. Through her use of abstract form and vivid palate, Uhler's *Decoration: Red Haw Trees* beautifully conveys the rich colors and mysterious forms of dense thickets that line the rivers and bayous that glide through the Houston landscape.

By 1929, the legendary E. M. (Buck) Schiwetz (1898–1984) had also moved to Houston to begin a painting and illustration career that would lead him across the entire state to draw and paint iconic images of the Texas scene. Schiwetz, an architect by training, chronicled the original architecture and landmark structures of cities and small towns throughout Texas. He frequently recorded the state's vast network of rivers, streams, and waterways that regularly flow across his wonderful watercolor and mixed media drawings. An early example is his superb watercolor *Main Street Viaduct*, featuring the bridge that then ran just beyond his studio.

Meanwhile, back in Dallas, Frank Reaugh, now recognized as one of the foremost painters in the American Southwest, maintained his prodigious output of impressionist masterpieces featuring Texas landscape and cattle. He continued to embed Texas rivers and streams into his landscape works. However, by the mid-1920s, two of Reaugh's young protégés were also making a name for themselves as formidable landscape painters in their own right. Edward Eisenlohr (1872–1961) and Reveau Bassett (1897–1981) were among Reaugh's most accomplished students and also among the first to become professionally successful as full-time artists. Both were ultimately selected for exhibition at the prestigious National Academy of Design, making them among the first Reaugh students to be so honored. Having been indoctrinated by Reaugh early in their careers, both artists maintained a deep fondness for the rivers, streams, and ponds feeding the North Texas expanses outside of Dallas, and both painted river subjects with acuity. Eisenlohr included the craggy creek beds or river bottoms around Dallas as frequent focal points of highly atmospheric, richly painted, impressionistic renderings. For his part, Bassett achieved notoriety for waterfowl and field hunting scenes, effectively becoming the state's first true wildlife artist. His paintings of rising and lighting waterfowl offer stunning presentations of the Texas river habitat that supported vast numbers of water birds on their annual migrations southward.

E. M. "Buck" Schiwetz, Main Street Viaduct, *1932, colored crayon on paper, 10¼ x 13¾ inches. Collection of Leila and Henri Gadbois*

Buffalo Bayou

Edward G. Eisenlohr, Cedar Creek, *ca. 1928, oil on canvas, 20 x 24 inches. Collection of Linda and Bill Reaves*

Cedar Creek, a tributary of the Trinity River

As the 1930s took hold, however, Impressionism was beginning to yield to other modes of painting in the Lone Star State, and forms of modernism were on the rise. In Dallas, a group of like-minded young artists embraced philosophical tenets and stylistic tendencies of American Regionalism, producing a series of ground-breaking works on the Texas scene. While the brand of Lone Star Regionalism practiced by the Dallas cohort may have represented a stylistic departure from their impressionist counterparts, their subject matter was no less embedded in the flora and fauna of local landscape, and Texas rivers remained paramount in their work. Artists like Alexandre Hogue (1898–1994), William Lester (1910–1991), and Everett Spruce (1908–2002) continued to explore the landscape, often recording river scenes in their expansive Regionalist repertoire. Alexandre Hogue, whose mid-1930s erosion series, executed at the height of the Texas Dust Bowl, would gain him fame and notoriety, was still making his way as an art instructor at a YMCA encampment in Glen Rose when he painted the distinctive rock formations found on the Paluxy River as it wound through the camp and through the adjacent Cross Tim-

Reveau Bassett, Ducks in Flight, Big Sandy, *ca. 1943, oil on canvas, 25¼ x 30 inches. Collection of Mr. and Mrs. M. G. Glasscock*

Big Sandy Creek, a tributary of the Sabine River

bers landscape. Ever sensitive to the plight of the land around him and cognizant of water-related issues, Hogue achieved prominence as one of Texas' (and America's) great Regionalist artists and, in doing so, became one of the first American artists to deliberately deploy his artwork in the cause of environmental activism.

William Lester hailed from Graham, Texas, and gained significant critical acclaim for his cubist-inspired surrealist modes of Texas land-

Alexandre Hogue, Paluxy Formations, *1927, oil on masonite, 12 x 16 inches. Collection of Mr. and Mrs. M. G. Glasscock*

Paluxy River

scapes. His 1942 view of the Trinity River titled *October on the Trinity* is demonstrative of his frequent attention to river subject matter as well as his interesting use of stylistic technique to accentuate the humid atmosphere and the corrosive interplay between land and water at the river's edge.

Also employing avant-garde style was Everett Spruce, who frequently conveyed the river's force in his abstract landscapes, incorporating fast-flowing streams and rocky-bottomed rivers early on to lend added dynamism and interesting geologic contrast to his distinctive cubist compositions. Spruce's mid-'30s landscape titled *West Texas Landscape* is an example of the artist's treatment of the movement of rivers in his earliest output.

Even as Regionalist style overtook Dallas in the '30s, there were prominent "holdouts" in Central Texas who continued to present the rivers and creeks of the Texas Hill Country in a more traditional manner. These artists focused on impressionist landscapes through the '40s, '50s, and '60s, becoming, in a sense, Texas' "second wave" of students of the Hill Country School and representing an extension of earlier schools of bluebonnet painters like Julian Onderdonk and José Arpa before them. Prominent among these second wave impressionists were Robert Wood (1889–1979), Porfirio Salinas (1910–1973), and Walton Leader (1876–1966), and together they produced many fine Texas river paintings.

Robert Wood was already a well-established artist when he came to San Antonio in the mid-1920s. He worked in the city until his move to California in 1941. During his tenure in the state, Wood established a strong following with his bluebonnet landscapes, but he also often included the Guadalupe and other rivers as subjects of his Texas paintings. In addition to his own work, Wood proved to be one of the early mentors of a young Porfirio Salinas.

As one of the state's most important Hispanic artists, Salinas showed rare, almost innate talent as a young painter, eventually becoming a favorite of Sam Rayburn, Lyndon Johnson, and other political and social elites. In his best works, Salinas is recognized today as one of the foremost Texas

William Lester, October on the Trinity, *1942, watercolor and gouache, 19 x 28 inches. George Newton Collection, courtesy of Russell Tether Fine Arts Assoc., LLC*

Trinity River

Everett Spruce, West Texas Landscape, *ca. 1938, oil on board, 22 x 28 inches. Collection of Jill and Jim Cochran*

unidentified river

landscape painters of the latter half of the twentieth century, and his treatment of Texas rivers in his earliest works is nothing short of spectacular.

Walton Leader was another prodigious landscape painter in and around the Austin area during the mid-century period. Of the latter twentieth-century Texas landscapists, Leader possibly painted Texas rivers and creeks more frequently than any of his counterparts, regularly incorporating the area's rocky-bottomed, slow-moving waters within his engaging Hill Country compositions.

Thus, the beauty and mystique of Texas rivers has lured landscape artists to their banks almost since the beginning, and in the annals of Texas art one need not search far to find incredible historical examples of river subject matter. These river subjects remain a hallmark within the oeuvres of many of our state's most accomplished landscape painters even today. Painters from every sector of the state still find the rivers around them compelling fodder for their brush. If anything, present-day output offers an even stronger and more varied look at the river's presence within the modern Texas scene, presenting painterly documentation of the state's

Robert Wood, Scene on the Guadalupe, *ca. 1940, oil on canvas, 25 x 30 inches. Collection of Bill and Eloise Blakeley*

Guadalupe River

Porfirio Salinas, The Pedernales River, *ca. 1950, oil on canvas, 20 x 24 inches. Collection of John H. Stone*

Pedernales River

lovely and diverse network of riverways and underscoring the special place and vital purpose that these treasured water sources still hold in the lives of twenty-first-century Texans.

The Continuing Legacy: Contemporary Views of Texas Rivers

For Texans like me, who respond to the visual depiction of the natural environment around them, the wealth of contemporary landscape painters may be counted among the many virtues of the Lone Star State today. Often undervalued within critical circles, landscape painters actually constitute a special breed of artists and represent important aesthetic and cultural assets in their own right. Unlike preceding generations of landscape painters who invented and perfected the genre within a period generally dominated by representational art forms, contemporary Texas painters have come of age amidst a dizzying maze of avant-garde styles, subjects, and compositional approaches through which to express their aesthetic points of view in paint. Thus, painters who pursue traditional landscapes today make a more conspicuous choice in defining their preferences to work in this particular realm than did earlier forebears of the late nineteenth and early twentieth century. It is a decision based upon an obvious appreciation of the Texas landscape itself as well as an appreciation of the legacy of Lone Star art. In that sense, today's Texas landscape painters continue to live out important regionalist ideals in their work, with the best of them assuming important roles as essential linchpins in the continued evolution of painting within the state. These artists consciously chose to paint places that are uniquely "Texas" and to paint them in a more or less traditional manner, albeit with their own unique voice and touch. In doing so, they perpetuate the efforts of artists before them to record on canvas the essence of what it means to be "Texan." They also paint the land and its rivers as they encounter them in their own time, and in doing this they help us to visually trace the ongoing natural transformations within our state—both past and present.

Fortunately for us, there are many outstanding landscape artists working today that continue to record Lone Star rivers all across the state. A sampling of twenty of the state's best contemporary artists are included here, along with their images addressing no fewer than fourteen Texas rivers, four of our innumerable creeks and bayous, and four of the lakes and estuaries that are integral to the immense river system of the Lone Star State.

Artist-Naturalists: Celebrating a River Habitat

Some of the most accomplished and prolific of today's Texas river painters approach the subject because they are simply as much environmentalists and naturalists as they are painters. Such is the case of the husband and wife duo of Margie Crisp and William Montgomery, who reside in the Central Texas town of Elgin. Elgin, of course, is far better known as a center for fine sausage than a center for fine art, and yet this tiny town quietly accommodates two of the state's best river painters. Well-traveled, well-trained, and well-established as exceptional painters and printmakers, these two professional artists have focused their individual and collective talents on the creation of visual tributes to some of Texas' most storied rivers—the Colorado and Nueces among them.

In 2013, channeling John Graves's epic trip along the Brazos, Margie Crisp undertook her own deeply personal journey down the Colorado river, tracing and documenting the life and lore along the river's banks and capturing its adjacent flora and fauna through a spectacular series of drawings, paintings, linocuts, and lithographs. Her experiences resulted in a full scale book (her first ever), titled *River of Contrasts: The Texas Colorado.*[6] It represents an extraordinary treatise on a Texas river, which she both wrote and illustrated. Receiving many of the state's most prestigious literary awards, the book proved Crisp is a compelling and insightful author and brought attention to her illustrations as nothing less than stunning works of art.

Crisp's drawings and prints of the Colorado reflect the refined eye, remarkable draftsmanship, and technical facility of a true master. Drawings, such as *Cliff Swallows* (page 66), literally offer a bird's-eye view of the river's meandering course through limestone cliffs and escarpments, revealing Crisp's marvelous compositional skills and compelling sense of perspective at work. In her Colorado lithos and lino-cuts, Crisp works in classic Regionalist style reminiscent of the work of earlier Texas printmakers, such as Alexandre Hogue, in an exquisite suite of linocuts depicting key ecosystems along the river. *Early Spring in the Basin* (page 67) is a prime example of this series. This work reflects the artist's engaging use of form and color in pleasing, slightly abstracted style and also demonstrates Crisp's exceptional control and stellar technical capacity as a printmaker.

Likewise, spouse William Montgomery is no stranger to the glories of Texas rivers in his own work. In *Fish Story I* (page 93), Montgomery portrays aquatic life on the Neches River in deep East Texas, and in doing so he demonstrates his own effectiveness as a painter as well as his knowledge as naturalist and outdoorsman. Through clever narrative embedded in the work, Montgomery reminds us of the river's incredible capacity to support bounties of reptiles, fish, and fowl as well as captures its enduring lure as playground for fishermen and other sportsmen. At the river's bottom, however, Montgomery also gently reminds us of the sad perils of human deposits on these otherwise pristine waterways, suggesting that we should further refrain from "messing with Texas" rivers as well. Collaborating with Crisp on an upcoming river project, Montgomery further applies his superb training and classical style to capture the fabled Nueces River. In a series of paintings that will illustrate this newest book on the Nueces River, Montgomery features the landscape and wildlife surrounding the river—the definitive water basin of South Texas. In *American Bitterns*, (page 92) Montgomery invokes Audubon-like style to capture the dynamic tension that exists today between the birds' native habitat and the manmade environment along the river's shores.

Fort Worth's Billy Hassell is yet another well-known artist-environmentalist whose repertoire and reputation transcend the bounds of Texas. A Dallas native with degrees from Notre Dame and the University of Massachusetts, Hassell is a devoted naturalist and a great river painter. He brings bold palettes and vibrant style to his distinctive visual chronicles of Lone Star wildlife and wildflowers, and he is especially fond of compositions that pair his wildlife subjects with the water habitat—rivers, lakes, bayous, or estuaries—that supports them. Paintings such as *Bend on the Brazos West of Weatherford* (page 82) are indicative of his active compositions and his penchant for color. Like several of his Texas contemporaries, Hassell offers hints of cubism in his Texas landscapes, composing his scenes on a relatively flat plane and favoring slightly stylized animal forms and natural structures similar to those found in earlier works of Otis Dozier (1904–1987) and other earlier Regionalist proponents of the '30s. His Devils River scene titled *Dolan Falls, Devils River* (page 83) shows these Regionalist proclivities and the exquisite results that he is able to achieve with this approach. Along with Crisp and Montgomery, Hassell is among a select group of Texas painters who lend their talent, as well as their artwork, to public initiatives in efforts to inspire and promote environmental activism and natural conservation within the state. Hassell has collaborated with groups such as the Nature Conservancy to supply art for the support of important environmental causes. Notable among these is his most recent series of color lithographs depicting wild things and wild places in Texas for the Texas Parks and Wildlife Foundation. This series includes his image of *Powderhorn Ranch* (page 84), which celebrates the state's acquisition of this incredible new wetlands reserve.

Painting the River in Pieces: Regional Interpretations of Texas Rivers

Goodbye to a River is one of the most significant books ever written on Texas soil.[7] In it, author John Graves suggests that entire river systems are complex constructs, often a quandary to get "arms around" in terms of visual impressions and personal interpretations. Texas rivers do indeed vary widely in their character, taking on distinctly different personalities and attributes as they traverse the state, and afford the artists who paint them entirely different views and perspectives depending upon the latitude and locales from which they are engaged. In describing the river's imagery, Graves aptly observes their grand deviations as follows:

> A whole river is mountain country and hill country and flat country and swamp and delta country, is rock bottom and sand bottom and weed bottom and mud bottom, is blue, green, red, clear, brown, wide, narrow, fast, slow, clean and filthy water, is all the kinds of trees and grasses and all the breeds of animals, birds and men that pertain and have ever pertained to its changing shores, is a thousand differing and not compatible things in-between that point where enough of the highland drainlets have trickled together to form it, and that wide, flat, probably desolate place where it discharges itself into the salt of the sea.[8]

Given the challenges of knowing rivers as a whole, Graves posits that these water sources can only be truly understood and appreciated by knowing them intimately, one piece at a time. This tenet would seem to hold particularly true and accurate for artists who seek to paint them with genuine affect and authenticity. As Texas rivers project their differing temperaments in long courses downstream, the landscape painter who paints them must, of necessity, adapt his or her own view, style, and approach to fit the rivers' mood and tone. The complexities of such ever-changing riverine personas account for the diversity in Texas river painting today and, indeed, represent one of the strongest arguments for river subjects as fertile, multidimensional strands in the artist's repertory. Getting to know the true nature of a river's parts enhances an artist's insights into the historic and geographic identity of his or her particular sectors of the state and, by observing the river's many moods, opens the door to virtually unlimited subject matter for the serious Texas landscape painter. Fortunately, today there are talented landscapists scattered throughout the entire state who seek to know the pieces of the Texas rivers immediately around them and who relish the water's transformative qualities as vital themes within their work.

In Marfa, for instance, there is Mary Baxter. This petite and affable artist works and resides in these outermost reaches of far West Texas in the majestic Big Bend country. She knows the Big Bend intimately, having come out many years ago as partner in a ranching venture there. Eventually trading in a cowgirl's spurs for canvas and brush, she proceeded to paint these storied environs with flourish and fidelity, translating the area's unique light, atmosphere, and geologic forms in elegant semi-abstracted landscapes. The few rivers that run through this remote corner of the state, the Rio Grande and Devils River, are never far from her daily life and thus never far from her canvas. She paints these Big Bend watersheds and their associated landscape with an elegance and sensitivity that can only be achieved through deep familiarity with the rivers' movements and affects.

In *Last Light Near Fresno Canyon* (page 62), Baxter paints the Rio Grande in early evening as it moves quietly through the high desert floor, fulfilling a role unknown to it as natural boundary between two lands and the cultures on either side. Using broad, simple strokes in straightforward composition, Baxter underscores the river's singular importance in this boundless country where its life-sustaining waters are equally welcomed and cherished by all things living, regardless of which side of the border they rest. In *Devils River, Downriver from West Bank* (page 60), the artist assumes a vantage point high above to show us the river's gentle wind through ribbons of colorful trees that line its banks in late afternoon. Baxter's paintings project Big Bend rivers in moody, transient tonality. Perhaps such transiency is simply characteristic of the shallow rivers as they ply through an American desert, with waters often so scarce and fleeting that light upon them can resonate in mysterious ways. Or perhaps it is because Baxter is able to integrate her rivers in perfect context with the land, using these streams of water to amplify the stark beauty and mysticism of the incredible Big Bend landscape. In any event, she knows these pieces of the rivers well and paints them with ardor and intrigue.

One moves only slightly upland from the Big Bend country to reach the high plains of the Llano Estacado or the sage brush prairies of West Texas. Several Texas rivers trace their sources from springs and underground aquifers there and run as networks of small tributaries into mainstream trunks that lead further down state. Painting river subjects on the West Texas plains requires the artist to chase the water's slow movement over sparse and tough expanses through narrow channels of red and yellow tones grooved out of sandstone skirts of painted earth. These small rivers, "drainlets" as Graves calls them, shed a cacophony of light, texture, color, and contour to these western sectors of the high plains. Fortunately, accomplished painters of the region "get it" and aptly capture the character of these West Texas rivers in art. One such West Texas artist is Albany painter Randy Bacon. Bacon left a successful Fort Worth advertising career several years ago to be closer to his boyhood roots in Abilene. Much like what A. C. Greene achieved through evocative prose, Bacon has somehow managed to do with paint, commandeering these parts of West Texas as a personal painting country and producing canvases that faithfully convey the area's spacious landscapes, large skies, and rural sensibilities. In *Double Mountain Fork of the Brazos* (page 56), he paints a shallow Brazos River pushing slowly through winding gorges carved from burnt orange subsoils. In this composition, Bacon beautifully conveys the river's lonely plight through an isolated landscape on to its destinations below to join the greater waters downstream.

Lubbock native Laura Lewis (recently of Mason) has also devoted herself to painting the high plains of West Texas, which she has known all her life. In *Brazos Clay* (page 89) and *North Pease River* (page 90), Lewis makes muscular use of heavy impasto to emphasize the undulating red clay bottoms and deep blue rivulets that are characteristic of these West Texas rivers. Lewis skillfully employs the river's bank as a stark horizon line upon which to rest the vast cobalt skies and titillating cloud formations that define this part of Texas.

Both Lewis and Bacon obviously appreciate the dynamic, broad panoramas that are afforded painters of this flat, expansive terrain, and they understand the dramatic geologic counterbalance that the river lends to composition as it cuts through wide open vistas. Bacon brings this point home in *Waldrip Bridge* (page 58) as he leads us visually to the edge of a precipice on the upper Colorado and invites us to cross an antique bridge in order to experience the full view of the river's reach in all directions. Likewise, in her painting entitled, *White River Watershed* (page 91), Lewis also shows us the benefits of the bigger view, emphasizing the river's just-out-of-sight presence as an ancient shapeshifting force and portraying its influence on the lay of lands all about it.

Accomplished landscape painters reside further downstream from these West Texas plateaus as well, waiting there to capture the rivers' changing views as they pick up speed and fleet across the rocky-bottomed streambeds at mid-state. From her Round Rock base, pastelist Jeri Salter makes a habit of painting the rivers that she encounters in frequent sketch trips deep into the Hill Country and well beyond, often ranging far out into the surrounding West Texas. With her ultra-proficient use of pastels, Salter is able to coax the myriad soft lights and delicate colors that manifest within the waters as they flow from the plains onto limestone beds of Hill Country terrain. *The Pecos at Pandale* (page 102) and *Last Light on San Gabriel River* (page 101) are examples of Salter's ability to capture the subtle interplay between earth, water, and light on the river's edge. In a grand morning vista titled *Brazos Sunrise at Village Bend* (page 100), Salter offers a sunlit morning glimpse of a graceful river as it bends through an ancient valley forged far below—a view that gives a clear sense of why this spot was treasured ground for the Comanche long before it was discovered by white settlers.

David Caton is surely one of the most significant Texas landscape artists working today. He lives close to the Frio in Utopia, Texas. He paints this river often, as well as other water sources about him, and when it comes to an accord with the rivers he paints, when all is said and done, Caton may just be the most important river painter of his era. He hails from Houston originally, and, after undergraduate training at the University of Houston and obtaining a master's degree in painting from Yale, he returned to the Texas Hill Country to fix his brush on the rugged landscape of that area (as well as the high desert vistas of the Big Bend).

Over the last twenty-five years, Caton has garnered high acclaim among Texas landscape artists. His well-executed compositions consistently yield stunning rough-country scenes, and these adorn the walls of countless private collections and corporate boardrooms. He is at his best, however, when painting water, a task representing no mean feat. It is one thing for an artist to paint a landscape with a river in it and yet something quite different for an artist to actually illuminate the flow of water streaming through the river itself. Dependent upon the times of day or year, the depths and surfaces below, and the atmosphere and light of the sky, water's movement within a river's flow can reflect thousands of hues and tones and vary in pace with the complexity of multivariate logarithms. Painting water well requires the artist to capture such nuanced variances as special effects in real time. Caton manages to capture these elusive attributes of water in his oil painting with virtual perfection, or at least with greater authenticity than almost anyone else.

The intrigue of water painting did not come lightly to the well-studied Caton, who found himself both inspired and mesmerized by a modest landscape painting titled *A Stream over Rocks*, done by American icon John Singer Sargent (1856–1925) in 1907. Encountering the work first at an exhibition at the Brooklyn Museum, Caton was sufficiently awed by the artist's fluency in painting the water's movement across a small brook that he forced himself to revisit the same work for further study on the two subsequent occasions when Sargent's painting appeared at museum exhibitions in Texas—at the McNay Museum in San Antonio and the Museum of Fine Arts Houston. These encounters with Sargent's small gem left Caton with dogged determination to achieve similar perfection with the rocky-bottomed rivers of his adopted Texas Hill Country, and he has pursued water as his muse ever since.

Fast Waters of the Rio Frio at Garner State Park (page 64) is illustrative of Caton's masterful treatment of the dynamic rush of the Frio as it gushes across the painting's mid-ground and exudes onto lower edges of the canvas, all the while dashing across dramatic rock forms amid the gleaming color fields embedded at the water's surface and just below. It is a remarkable work, worthy of holding any museum wall, perhaps beside Sargent's equally fine rendition.

While *Fast Waters* is a tribute to the movement and energy of a Texas river, in *Botkin Ranch* (page 63), Caton presents a tour-de-force of the water's multiple moods in complex, three-tiered composition. In this painting of a spot near his home on North Little Creek, Caton captures the creek's top waters in peaceful repose, gliding slow and green in a sunlit background. Closer in, at mid-ground, these same waters reappear in silver-blue streams and rapid cadence as they free-fall down a limestone drop, only to emerge yet again in the lower foreground as a crystal-clear, gently running pool—the entire transformation harmoniously achieved and completely soothing to the eye.

It was, however, the disturbing absence of waters in these Central Texas rivers that drew Austin photographer Robb Kendrick to cover the great drought of 2011–2012 for *National Geographic* magazine. Kendrick, an insightful photographer and child of the Texas Panhandle, has traveled the world extensively, developing photographic essays for the esteemed magazine of popular geography. In between his international photoshoots for *National Geographic*, the independent photographer fed his inherent Texas sensibilities through time spent on prominent Texas ranches documenting the life and work of contemporary cowboys with ingenious use of archaic tin-type photographic techniques. Kendrick's tin-types resulted in a pair of notable and highly acclaimed books adding a much-needed twenty-first century update to the mystique of the American cowboy. Thus aware of the parched Texas ranchlands, Kendrick relished *National Geographic*'s bid for him to turn his lens toward the devastating effects of the great twenty-first century drought in Central and West Texas. His sobering image of *San Saba River, Voca, Texas* (page 88) shows the desolate limestone base of a river once streaming with cool, blue-green waters on their move across the hills now completely ravaged by the great drought.

This river work, and indeed Kendrick's entire drought series, represents a stunning, yet horrific, photographic essay on the traumatic stresses that this river, and indeed, the entire water system of the state, has had to overcome recently.

Further south, artists have opportunity to study the rivers' character as they flow closer to their ultimate destinations into the Gulf of Mexico. Corpus Christi artist Noe Perez, a native of Falfurrias in the South Texas brush country, is among the few artists able to actualize the deep, understated beauty of this sector. Capitalizing upon what can only be an innate artistic ability, the self-taught Perez, a professional engineer by training, works with incredible acuity and paints his South Texas homelands with an allegiant sincerity. His tenacious pursuit of excellence has resulted in impressionist works that are superbly composed, presenting incomparable motifs of Gulf plains and South Texas pasturelands. His works, especially those containing the blooming prickly pears so prominent in the vicinity, are eagerly sought by Texas collectors. His is an area rich in character and home to historic, far-flung Texas ranching empires presided over by O'Connors, Kings, Kenedys, and Armstrongs. To approach his native painting grounds, Perez passes across remnants of these old ranch lands, which span collections of muddy creeks and murky rivers that slice through the country and eventually drain into wetlands and estuaries feeding the bays below. This can be tough, unforgiving country for a painter to paint, sparse and lush at the same time, but Perez's acquaintance with and affinity for the landscape enables him to capture the nuanced elegance of it all. Such can be seen in his late afternoon scene along Santa Gertrudis Creek (*Una Manana en el Arroya Santa Gertrudis*, page 96) as the sun begins to recede and evening approaches the meandering stream of water. Likewise, in *Coastal Oaks II* (page 98), Perez captures stately coastal oaks regally posed along the shores of Aransas Bay, bathed in spring-fed light. While especially adept at painting his South Texas homelands, Perez's prowess as a river painter is not limited to that locale, as evidenced in his beautiful execution of *River Road View* (page 99), an extraordinary interpretation of the Rio Grande crossing through Big Bend National Park.

Finding Texas at the River's End: The Nexus of Nature and History

A bit north and east of Perez country takes one deeper into coastal stomping grounds shared by Debbie Stevens (of Cypress) and Lee Jamison (of Huntsville), two Southeast Texas artists who regularly ply these areas close to the rivers' end in search of historical landmarks or coastal wildlife materials for their incredible works. To work here, these artists experience the bayous and great rivers as they present themselves in coastal counties at the end of their long journeys, engorged to their broadest, deepest, and sometimes their most dangerous and foreboding points. Of necessity, coastal artists such as Jamison and Stevens must observe the bottom lands and waters about them with added care and caution, which, in turn, heightens artistic awareness and opens them to some of the most interesting, diverse, and contemplative scenery that Texas rivers can reveal.

Jamison is a historical painter and, as such, is constantly in search of the vestiges of times past that still stand, albeit obscured, within our midst. The river bottoms spreading across old Austin land grants in coastal Texas are replete with the history and artifacts of local industry and culture, and Jamison approaches these low-lying waterways as "happy hunting grounds" for his historical surveys. *Lynchburg Ferry* (page 86) is an example of Jamison's ability to mix good art with good history. It is a beautifully composed painting with water and skies showered in the blue-gold embers of evening sunlight, setting the historic Lynchburg Ferry (still operating today) against a backdrop of the San Jacinto monument. As Jamison does better than almost anyone, this painting seamlessly ties past and present together, inviting reflections on the river's longtime role as a central byway in the lives of the surrounding populous and the travails of Texas history. In *The Light of Industry, Freeport* (page 87), Jamison paints a beautiful nocturne of the "Old Brazos" in Freeport, conveying an evening of peaceful balance among interests of industry, sportsmen, and river life. In subtle visual narrative, Jamison's scene underscores the river's vital role in accommodating the varied needs of each. Sporting full-fledged impressionist technique, Jamison's powerful waterscape, titled *Evening Sun and Spanish Moss (Off the Sabine River)* (page 85), does all its talking in deep color and graceful forms to convey the artist's admonition on the importance and grandeur of the swamp lands and tidal basins that are slowly vanishing from coastal lowlands of Southeast Texas.

While Jamison concentrates on the human history and industrial footprints (or lack thereof) on these coastal rivers, Debbie Stevens portrays the native birdlife that inhabits them. As did Audubon those many years before, Stevens still searches out and documents the splendid species of the large water birds that populate the lower Texas coast. To do so, she must pursue her subjects in natural surroundings, and thus she and husband Jerry travel often to the area's many coastal inlets, bays, and adjacent wildlife preserves, securing photographic reference material of pelicans, cranes, herons, egrets, spoonbills, and more. The resultant paintings are a joy to behold, garnering Stevens with critical plaudits as well as regular invitations to many of the nation's most prestigious wildlife painting forums. Her compositions are exquisitely painted with sublime brushwork and Vermeer-like tonality. In works like *Roseate Splendor 2* (page 105) and *Elusive Beauty* (page 106), Stevens packs her combination of photorealism and abstraction into distinctive waterfowl paintings, rendering her subject birdlife in stunning detail and then positioning these majestic birds on planes of shimmering waters made naturally abstract by virtue of reflected light across the rivulets. The effect is quite unique and genuinely lovely in form. Similar to David Caton, Stevens's treatment of moving water, while different than Caton's approach, adds to the allure of her riverscapes and distinguishes her as a water painter of the highest order.

City Views and Sophisticated Style: Modernist Interpretations of Life and Lore on Texas Rivers

While Texas rivers offer strong subject matter downstream on deltas and bottomlands, many of these same rivers and bayous roll first through inland towns and cities. Enhancing their appointed cities with a visual opulence and sense of quiet refuge, these rivers do not escape the eyes of city-borne artists. As case in point, consider how Buffalo Bayou forms the perfect backdrop for the architectural portraits that Charles Ford (1941–2016) paints of popular landmarks on the Houston scene. His twin views of *Buffalo Bayou at the Jackson Hill Bridge* (page 74) and *Buffalo Bayou at Waugh Drive* (page 76) trace the Bayou's course downstream as it saunters through man-made cliffs of high rise architecture. As city planners and landscape architects have obviously already discovered, water seems to only enhance accompanying architectural elements surrounding it, and so it is with Ford's architectural paintings. In a contemplative, metaphysical manner, Fort Worth painter Pat Gabriel captures the moody presence of the Trinity River's flow across the urban flood plains of Cow Town beneath high banks of billowing clouds in a painting simply titled *Trinity* (page 77). Besides being an incredibly beautiful painting of a placid urban moment, Gabriel's view of the Trinity, with its undisturbed waters crossing unrequited planes, is allegorical in nature, invoking thoughtful reflection on matters of past, present, and future. The paintings of these artists underscore the powerful place of rivers in the urban environment of contemporary society, as both sources of enhanced beauty and as catalysts for quiet reflection on the higher meanings of hasty lives.

There are, of course, contemporary Texas artists who choose to interpret Lone Star rivers with more robust and imaginative style. One, for instance, would be Keith Davis, a self-taught Texas painter who is every bit as creative and colorful as his whimsical paintings. Originally a flatlander from Levelland, Texas, Davis found his way into the capital city several years ago, eventually landing a permanent home studio in an East Austin arts center. There he churns out bright and colorful renditions of the Texas topography, featuring an array of iconic critters and engaging characters. As an avowed Austinite now, Davis views the Colorado River running through his town not unlike many Austinites do—as a public accoutrement for recreation and entertainment. *Fishing on Town Lake at Sunset with Bats* (page 70) perfectly captures Davis's manner of river painting. In this work he playfully conveys, as he always does, the triumph of the regular guy. In this case, Davis introduces a proud but lonesome fisherman, sitting tall and smugly displaying the just rewards of a long day's fishing on Lady Bird Lake. Behind him, as a stream of bats disembarks from dark roosts under the Congress Street Bridge, Davis further reveals important clues as to the time and location of the subject episode, giving the viewer the necessary bearings of this fisherman's delight just in case they want to try their own luck at the same spot. Likewise, in *Tubing Down the Guadalupe* (page 71), the artist paints up another scene of frolic on the Texas riverfront. Here, of course, Davis's spry group of tubers is embarking upon one of summer's greatest natural experiences—a wet and wild journey down a fast-moving Hill Country stream. As a self-taught artist, Davis maintains the rare, latent ability to paint "fun" into every work he produces and, in creating such fanciful river scenes, he reminds us again of the simple pleasures and natural revelry offered by Texas rivers to those who simply venture out and avail themselves.

Richardson painter Jon Flaming also applies bright color and compelling style to capture the essence of Texas rivers. Similar to Davis, he imbues *Bridge Over the Brazos* (page 73) with inherent joy, perfectly capturing the charm and nostalgia of an older generation of antique highway bridges and low-water crossings that still populate the Lone Star backcountry if only one is inclined to pursue them off of interstate thoroughfares. In what has been described as Neo-Regionalism in style, Flaming's works, such as in this grand composition, pay homage to ghosts of the Dallas Nine. With vivid colors and cubistic structures, the artist juxtaposes his welcoming "bridge-less-traveled" with a menagerie of hearty creatures and lush plant life that share this special passage across the iconic river. Flaming's work always asks us to reconsider the simple beauties of the Texas outback, and, in this, he reminds us how Texas rivers still pervade our modern-day visions of the sublimity found in rural retreats.

William Young is yet another artist who paints his Texas rivers with more playful perspective, yet he goes even further to add the additional dimension of surrealism. In his river paintings, Young imagines the native wildlife as a cast of indigenous actors and employs the adjoining landscape as theatric backdrop through which to play out important tales and folklore concerning the rivers' history and culture. He comes by these surrealistic tendencies quite naturally, having tutored with his own artist-father, Ancil Nunn (1928–1999), who was among the best to ever work this sophisticated genre within the state. In paintings such as *The Source of the Brazos* (page 109), Young further enriches the Brazos River lore by ingeniously ascribing the river's mysterious source to an industrious scissortail fly-catcher with a single old tea kettle. (Likely this is not the true source of the river, but it makes for captivating narrative nonetheless!) In his painting titled *Outlaws at Rock Crossing on the Red River* (page 108), Young spins yet another river yarn about robber's loot pilfered from a North Texas bank and buried by a band of cunning outlaws, played by a pack of conniving coyotes in cowboy suits, on the banks of the Red River. Like Davis and Flaming, Young shows us that painting Texas rivers can actually be an especially inventive and fun-filled exercise for those artists who work with creative flair.

Water Works: Watercolor Interpreters of Texas Rivers

A discussion of river painting would be incomplete without consideration of the river's treatment by those artists who prefer to do their paintings in water-based media. Houston is home to an active society of watercolor artists, and among that group, two veteran painters stand out for their exquisite renderings of Texas rivers through use of the watercolor media. Erik Sprohge and Hunter George are the two accomplished and award-winning watercolorists referenced here. Both gentlemen now paint after long and successful professional careers in architecture and advertising, respectfully. Following in the footsteps of the inimitable Buck Schiwetz, both share Schiwetz's affinity for capturing classic elements of the Texas scene, including its river places, in water-based media. While Sprohge and George are equally adept in their use and command of this most challenging of media, their approaches to imagery and watercolor applications are entirely their own.

Erik Sprohge's *Evening Walk* (page 103) of late afternoon on Buffalo Bayou set under flaming sunset skies is an incredible mood study, showing the bayou's pastoral side with a welcoming church next to a favored evening walking path. Sprohge demonstrates his strength as composer, as well as colorist, in this rich watercolor painting that extends a visual invitation for the viewer to join the walk. In *River Rock* (page 104), Sprohge capitalizes upon the mass and semi-abstract qualities of a single granite boulder marooned in the fast-running waters of the Guadalupe River. In a remarkable feat of watercolor magic, Sprohge paints this inanimate stone in exquisite portrait style, beautifully conveying its strong form and sturdy presence in the path of the river's waters and amplifying the ambient light, variant color, and rich texture that are prominent in the subject.

Hunter George explores the back roads of Central Texas in frequent excursions and respites into the Hill Country. There, he still finds nostalgic settings worthy of sketch notes in his watercolor journals. The best of these studies he returns to convert into exquisite full-scale watercolor renderings. In the case of *Lange's Mill at Doss, TX* (page 81), George records the remnants of an old mill in Doss, a Hill Country landmark and relic of an earlier time when the force of Threadgill Creek off the Llano River was employed to mill and grind the grain crops of the area's hard-scrabble farms. In *Crossing the Guadalupe* (page 80), George remembers for us the marvel and grandeur of old railroad engines that once pushed through massive iron bridges crisscrossing the rivers within the state. Both those trains and river bridges represented astounding engineering advances only decades ago. In his nostalgic rural river scenes, George gives us the remote markers of enterprise far away from the big Texas cities and reminds us of the longstanding need and ingenuity to ford the river's void and conquer its resources for causes of commerce and industry.

Silent Metaphors: The Messianic Realm of Texas Rivers

Perhaps the oldest and most revered symbolism of rivers in art, as well as scripture, is found in their metaphorical use as great divides over which passage delivers the promise of renewed life and better prospects. Pat Gabriel's *Trinity* (page 77) teases with these precepts, luring us onto a placid plane and extending our thoughts onward to consider the prospects and possibilities of the lands and clouds across the river beyond. In Gabriel's work, of course, the river's crossing is only imagined, and whether one crosses or not, and what is to be found even if one should cross are truly in the eyes of the beholder. However, in *The Crossing* (page 72), a powerful scene painting by Austin artist Fidencio Duran, the aftermath of a true river passage is sensitively portrayed in rich human perspective. Duran's scene depicts the actual crossing of his parents over the Rio Grande into Texas during the time of consolidation after the Mexican Revolution (1920–1940). Using skillful narrative, Duran paints the river as merely a meager line in the painting's background, overcome and overshadowed instead by noble figures in a captivating foreground, posing the modest couple in deep and climactic emotions upon crossing over the river's banks. The pair exalts the moment, praying to greater angels in gratitude for renewed opportunity and safe harbor. Duran's scene is forceful and beautifully rendered. While a personal homage to his own family's experience, Duran's subject obviously resonates with poignant contemporary meaning as well, as such hopeful crossings by those seeking prosperity and refuge remain paramount today, authorized or not. It is only one way in which the draw of Texas rivers continues in our lives.

As Andrew Sansom notes in his contribution to this book, the rivers of Texas have always been inextricably bound to the development and destiny of the people who have inhabited the state. These rivers have also wound their way into the imaginations, lives, and art of all Texans. The artists featured in this book are only the latest to be deeply affected by Texas rivers; the wildlife that lives on, around, and in them; and the irresistible call they exert.

It is our hope, as well as that of the artists featured in this book, that Texans will continue to relish such sumptuous imagery of our state's rivers. We also hope that Texans will never forget that the beauty we cherish in the natural world is intimately connected to our ability and willingness to be good stewards of these resources.

Notes

1. Kevin J. Avery, Oswaldo Rodriguez Roque, John K. Howat, Doreen Bolger Burke, and Catherine Hoover Voosanger, *American Paradise: The World of the Hudson River School* (New York: Metropolitan Museum of Art, 1987).

2. Texas Parks and Wildlife Foundation: Celebrating 25 Years (Austin: Texas Parks and Wildlife Foundation, 2016).

3. Pauline A. Pinckney, *Painting in Texas: The Nineteenth Century*, (Austin: University of Texas Press, 1967), 43–49.

4. James Patrick McGuire, Hermann Lungkwitz, *Romantic Landscapist on the Texas Frontier* (Austin, University of Texas Press, 1984).

5. Cecilia Steinfeldt, *The Onderdonks: A Family of Painters* (San Antonio: Trinity University Press, 1975) 9–59.

6. Margie Crisp, *River of Contrasts: The Texas Colorado* (College Station: Texas A&M University Press, 2012).

7. John Graves, *Goodbye to a River* (New York: Knopf, 1960).

8. Ibid, p. 4.

Featured Art

Randy Bacon, Double Mountain Fork of the Brazos. *2012, oil on canvas, 26 x 72 inches. Collection of BNSF Railway*

Brazos River

Randy Bacon, The Bridges at Samuels Avenue. *2009, oil on canvas, 38 x 80 inches. Collection of Bob Black and Gary Tucker*

Trinity River

Randy Bacon, Waldrip Bridge. *2015, oil on canvas, 17 x 72 inches. Collection of Jody Klotz*

Colorado River

OPPOSITE PAGE: *Mary Baxter,* Devils River, Downriver from West Bank. *2016, oil on ceconite, 48 x 40 inches. WRFA Collection of Janet Chavigny*

Devils River

Mary Baxter, Dolan Falls. *2016, oil on paper, 24 x 20 inches. Courtesy of William Reaves | Sarah Foltz Fine Art*

Devils River

Mary Baxter, Last Light Near Fresno Canyon. *2014, oil on polyfiber, 42 x 32 inches. Courtesy of William Reaves | Sarah Foltz Fine Art*

Rio Grande

David Caton, Botkin Ranch. *2015, oil on canvas, 40 x 60 inches. Courtesy of William Reaves | Sarah Foltz Fine Art*

North Little Creek, near Frio River

David Caton, Fast Waters of Rio Frio at Garner State Park. *2014, oil on canvas, 48 x 48 inches. The Bobbie and John L. Nau Collection of Texas Art*

Frio River

David Caton, Toward Mule Ears from the Mouth of Santa Elena. *2014, oil on canvas, 48 x 48 inches. Collection of John H. Stone*

Rio Grande

Margie Crisp, Cliff Swallows. *2002, charcoal on paper, 44 x 30 inches. Collection of Neil L. Chavigny and Mary K. Baxter*

Colorado River

Margie Crisp, Early Spring in the Basin. *2009, hand-colored linocut, 17 x 22.5 inches. Courtesy of William Reaves | Sarah Foltz Fine Art*

Colorado River

Margie Crisp, New World. *2011, hand-colored linocut, 17 x 22.5 inches. Courtesy of William Reaves | Sarah Foltz Fine Art*

Colorado River

Margie Crisp, River Dock at Night. *2011, lithograph, 3.25 x 4.5 inches. Collection of Leslie Thompson*

Colorado River

Keith Davis, Fishing on Town Lake at Sunset with Bats. *2015, oil on canvas, 24 x 18 inches. Courtesy of William Reaves | Sarah Foltz Fine Art*

Colorado River

Keith Davis, Tubing Down the Guadalupe. *2015, oil on canvas, 24 x 18 inches. Courtesy of William Reaves | Sarah Foltz Fine Art*

Guadalupe River

Fidencio Duran, The Crossing. *2005, oil on canvas, 18 x 18 inches. Private Collection, Houston*

Rio Grande

Jon Flaming, Bridge Over the Brazos. *2013, oil on canvas, 48 x 36 inches. Collection of Neil L. Chavigny and Mary K. Baxter*

Brazos River

Charles Ford, Buffalo Bayou at the Jackson Hill Bridge. *2015, acrylic on Masonite, 24 x 32 inches. Courtesy of William Reaves | Sarah Foltz Fine Art*

Buffalo Bayou

AIG

AT LEFT: *Charles Ford,* Buffalo Bayou at Waugh Drive. *2015, acrylic on masonite, 32 x 24 inches. Courtesy of William Reaves | Sarah Foltz Fine Art*

Buffalo Bayou

Pat Gabriel, Trinity. *2015, oil on canvas, 24 x 65 inches. Courtesy of William Reaves | Sarah Foltz Fine Art*

Trinity River

Pat Gabriel, Wet Wash (Near the Trailhead of McKittrick Canyon). *2013, oil on canvas, 8 x 21 inches. Collection of BNSF Railway*

McKittrick Canyon, near the Delaware River

Gabriel '13

Hunter George, Crossing the Guadalupe. *2003, watercolor, 12 x 16 inches. Courtesy of William Reaves | Sarah Foltz Fine Art*

Guadalupe River

Hunter George, Langes Mill at Doss, TX. *2013, watercolor, 16 x 22 inches. Courtesy of William Reaves | Sarah Foltz Fine Art*

Threadgill Creek, near Llano River

Billy Hassell, Bend on the Brazos West of Weatherford. *2016, oil on canvas, 36 x 80 inches. Courtesy of William Reaves | Sarah Foltz Fine Art*

Brazos River

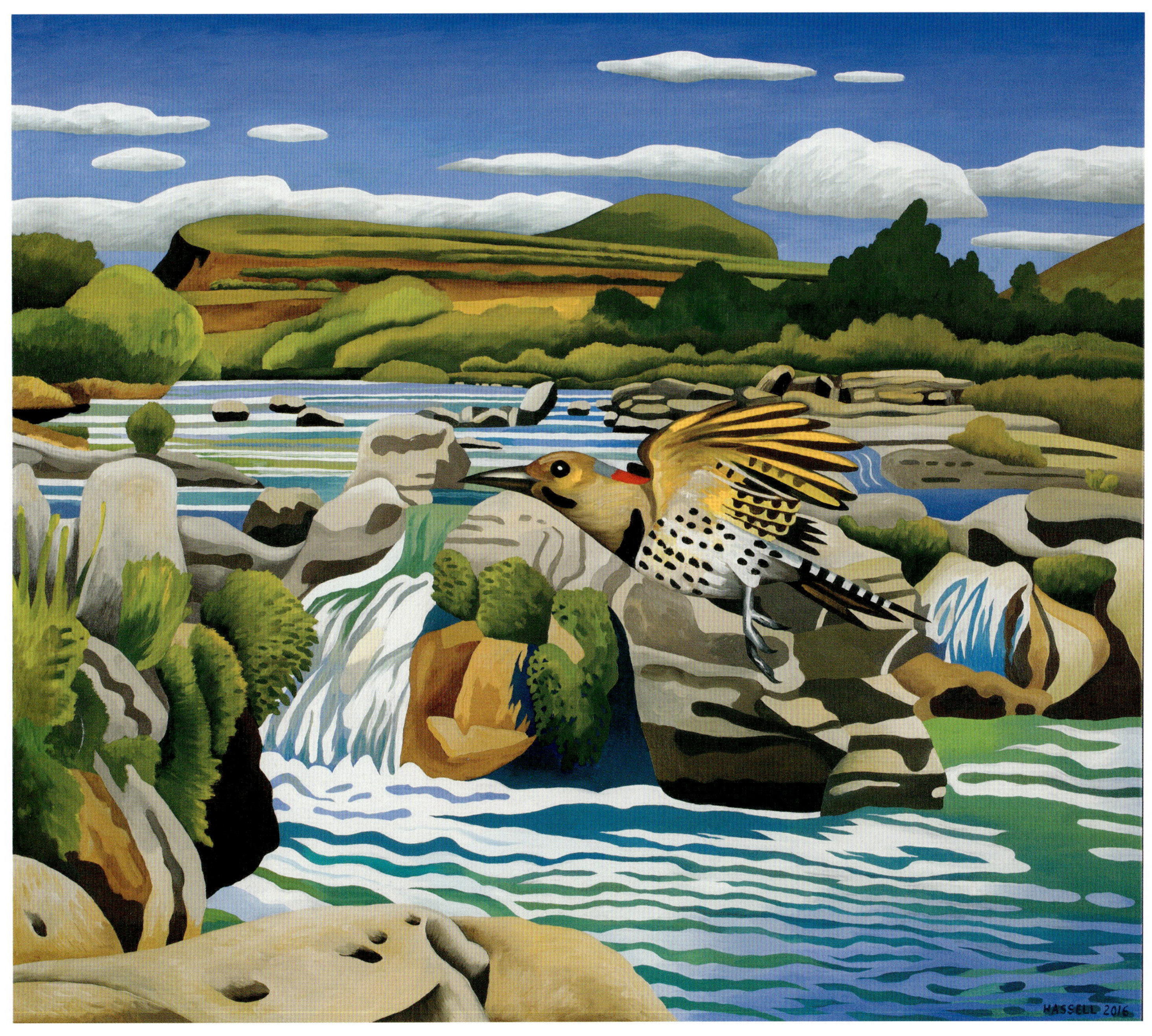

Billy Hassell, Dolan Falls, Devils River. *2016, oil on canvas, 36 x 40 inches. Courtesy of William Reaves | Sarah Foltz Fine Art*

Devils River

Billy Hassell, Powderhorn Ranch. *2015, lithograph, 24 x 22 inches. Courtesy of William Reaves | Sarah Foltz Fine Art*

Gulf Coast, near Matagorda Bay

Lee Jamison, Evening Sun and Spanish Moss (Off the Sabine River). *2015, oil on canvas, 24 x 48 inches. Courtesy of William Reaves | Sarah Foltz Fine Art*

Sabine River

Lee Jamison, Lynchburg Ferry. *2015, oil on canvas, 30 x 40 inches. Courtesy of William Reaves | Sarah Foltz Fine Art*

San Jacinto River/Houston Ship Channel

Lee Jamison, The Light of Industry, Freeport. *2015, oil on canvas, 36 x 48 inches. Courtesy of William Reaves | Sarah Foltz Fine Art*

Brazos River

Robb Kendrick, San Saba River, Voca, Texas. *2011, archival print, 18 x 22 inches. Courtesy of William Reaves | Sarah Foltz Fine Art*

San Saba River

Laura Lewis, Brazos Clay. *2012, oil on panel, 34 x 32 inches. Courtesy of William Reaves | Sarah Foltz Fine Art*

Brazos River

Laura Lewis, North Pease River. *2013, oil on canvas, 40 x 40 inches. Collection of Frank Klein*

Pease River

Laura Lewis, White River Watershed. *2010, oil on canvas, 60 x 90 inches. Courtesy of William Reaves | Sarah Foltz Fine Art*

White River

William Montgomery, American Bitterns. *2014, oil on canvas, 36 x 48 inches. Courtesy of William Reaves | Sarah Foltz Fine Art*

Nueces River

William Montgomery, Fish Story I. *2013, oil on canvas, 36 x 50 inches. Collection of Mr. and Mrs. M. G. Glasscock*

Neches River

William Montgomery, Tropical Parulas on Pulliam Creek. *2013, oil on canvas, 20 x 26 inches. Collection of Mr. and Mrs. M. G. Glasscock*

Pulliam Creek, near Nueces River

William Montgomery, Upper Nueces, East Fork. *2014, oil on canvas, 36 x 42 inches. Courtesy of William Reaves | Sarah Foltz Fine Art*

Nueces River

Noe Perez, Una Mañana en el Arroyo Santa Gertrudis. *2016, oil on canvas, 24 x 48 inches. Collection of Jody and Jamey Clement*

Santa Gertrudis Creek, near the Nueces River

Noe Perez, Coastal Oaks II. *2016, oil on canvas, 20 x 30 inches. Collection of Janet Chavigny*

Aransas Bay

Noe Perez, River Road View. *2011, oil on canvas, 24 x 48 inches. Collection of Andrew and Nona Sansom*

Rio Grande

Jeri Salter, Brazos Sunrise at Village Bend. *2014, pastel, 18 x 29.5 inches. Collection of Nancy Powell Moore*

Brazos River

Jeri Salter, Last Light on San Gabriel River. *2015, pastel on panel, 20 x 30 inches. Courtesy of William Reaves | Sarah Foltz Fine Art*

San Gabriel River

Jeri Salter, The Pecos at Pandale. *2015, pastel on panel, 18 x 30 inches. Courtesy of William Reaves | Sarah Foltz Fine Art*

Pecos River

Erik Sprohge, Evening Walk. *2009, watercolor, 10 x 14 inches. Courtesy of William Reaves | Sarah Foltz Fine Art*

Buffalo Bayou

Erik Sprohge, River Rock. *2009, watercolor, 19 x 27 inches. Courtesy of William Reaves | Sarah Foltz Fine Art*

Guadalupe River

Debbie Stevens, Roseate Splendor 2. *2011,*
oil on canvas, 36 x 72 inches.
Private Collection

Trinity Bay

Debbie Stevens, Elusive Beauty. *2014, oil on canvas, 18 x 36 inches. Courtesy of William Reaves | Sarah Foltz Fine Art*

Harris County coastal marshes

Debbie Stevens, Peaceful Journey. *2016, oil on canvas, 18 x 36 inches. Courtesy of William Reaves | Sarah Foltz Fine Art*

Gulf coast, near Matagorda Bay

William Young, Outlaws at Rock Crossing on the Red River. *2013, acrylic on masonite, 23 x 28 inches. Collection of Neil L. Chavigny and Mary K. Baxter*

Red River

William Young, The Source of the Brazos. *2009, acrylic on masonite, 18 x 24 inches.*
Private Collection

Brazos River

ABOUT THE ARTISTS

Randy Bacon (b. 1957, Abilene, Texas)

Randy Bacon currently resides and works in Albany, Texas. He studied studio art at the University of Texas at Austin and earned his bachelor of fine arts degree in studio art and journalism from Southern Methodist University. Before choosing painting as his true vocation, Bacon was president of Stuart Bacon Advertising and Public Relations in Fort Worth, a full-service agency he cofounded with Jim Stuart.

During a summer fellowship in painting at the Vermont Studio Center, Bacon had the opportunity to improve his skill and develop his personal style. His decision to return to painting full time followed. Continuing to grow as an artist, Bacon was awarded a full scholarship at Texas Christian University, where he earned his master of fine arts degree in painting.

Randy Bacon has always been attracted to the quality of light, the precise colors, and the big skies of his native state. In communicating a sense of place, Bacon often draws upon the people and venues of his life to bring about work where past, present, and future become blended, where memory and reality connect.

SELECTED BIOGRAPHICAL AND CAREER HIGHLIGHTS

1976–77 Studio Art, University of Texas at Austin
1980 BFA, Studio Art and Journalism, Southern Methodist University, Dallas
2003 Fellowship in painting, Vermont Studio Center, Johnson, Vermont
2007 MFA, Painting, Texas Christian University, Fort Worth
2007 Finalist, Hunting Art Prize Competition
Resides in Albany, Texas

SELECTED EXHIBITIONS

2007 *The Artist's Eye,* Kimbell Art Museum, Fort Worth
2007 *Hunting Art Prize Exhibition*, Houston
2007 Solo, Grace Museum, Abilene

2007 *The Texas Five*, Museum of East Texas Culture, Palestine

2007–09 *Cherry Spring Arts Festival*, Cherry Spring

2007–12 *Annual Invitational*, Panhandle-Plains Historical Museum, Canyon

2008–12 *Preservation is the Art of the City*, Fort Worth Community Arts Center, Fort Worth

2009 Solo, *A Cell of One's Own*, The Old Jail Art Center, Albany

2009 *Trinity Perspectives, Views of an Urban River*, Fort Worth Community Arts Center, Fort Worth

2010 *Art of the Red River War: A Clash of Cultures on the Southern Plains*, Panhandle-Plains Historical Museum, Canyon

2010 *Drawing on the Past: Selections from the Bobbie and John Nau Collection of Texas Art*, Grace Museum, Abilene

2011–12 Solo, *Familiar Territory: The Art of Randy Bacon*, National Ranching Heritage Center, Texas Tech University, Lubbock

2012 *Contemporary Texas Regionalists*, traveled: Haley Memorial Library & History Center, Midland; Gage Hotel, Marathon

2012 Solo, *Randy Bacon: The Colors of West Texas*, William Reaves Fine Art, Houston

2013 *Restless Heart: Contemporary Texas Regionalism*, San Angelo Museum of Fine Arts, San Angelo (cataloge)

2013 *Celebrating the Regionalist Legacy in Texas Art*, William Reaves Fine Art and the San Angelo Museum of Fine Arts at the Gage Hotel, Marathon

2013 *Holidays at the Haley*, Haley Memorial Library & History Center, Midland

2014–15 *Painting in the Texas Tradition*, traveled: Turner House, Dallas; Pearl Fincher Museum of Fine Arts, Spring (catalog)

2015 *Ties that Bind: Contemporary Texas Regionalism*, Turner House, Dallas

2015 *Texas Visions: Contemporary Texas Regionalism*, Nave Museum, Victoria

2015 *As Far as the Eye Can See: 100 Years of Texas Art*, Two Allen Center, Houston

SELECTED PUBLIC COLLECTIONS

Baldwin Anthony Securities Inc., Dallas

Burlington Northern Santa Fe, Santa Fe, New Mexico

First Financial Bank, Abilene
Happy State Bank, Amarillo
Grace Museum, Abilene
Mansefeldt Corporation, Abilene
Moncrief Oil, Fort Worth
Waterford Capital, Dallas
Woodbine Development Corporation, Dallas

Mary Baxter (b. 1963, Lubbock, Texas)

Mary Baxter has always had a keen interest in art, particularly as a result of family camping trips to the Chihuahuan Desert. She pursued her passion at the University of Texas at San Antonio, where she studied painting and advanced printmaking and earned her bachelor of science degree. Fully self-financing her studies, Baxter worked across the country on the high goal polo circuit.

Baxter moved to the Big Bend region when she leased a ranch Southwest of Marfa for raising cattle and training horses. It was there that she began to see the beauty of the rugged desert and interpret it in her paintings. After several years, she was able to free herself of ranch duties to paint full time.

She relocated to Marathon and opened the Baxter Studio and Gallery in the old Shoemake Hardware Building. There, she continued to produce and sell her works for ten years. Baxter currently resides and works in Marfa, using a vintage Silver Streak trailer to live in more remote locations where she creates some of her smaller, plein air paintings. She frequently gathers ideas and sketches for larger pieces that she finishes later in her studio. This approach has helped Baxter truly convey the beauty of the Texas landscape.

SELECTED BIOGRAPHICAL AND CAREER HIGHLIGHTS

1988 BS, Painting and Advanced Printmaking, University of Texas at San Antonio
2002–12 Baxter Studio and Gallery, Marathon
2005 Best in Show, *Trappings of Texas*, Museum of the Big Bend, Alpine
2006–07 Residency, McDonald Observatory, Fort Davis

2008 Finalist, Hunting Art Prize Competition
2011 Residency, Madroño Ranch, Medina
Resides in Marfa, Texas

SELECTED EXHIBITIONS

2003 Solo, Ballroom Marfa
2004 Five-person show, Baxter Gallery, Marathon
2005 Two-person show, Highland Gallery, Marfa
2005–08 *Trappings of Texas*, Museum of the Big Bend, Alpine
2005–09 *Annual Animal Art Show*, Invitational, Big Bend Venue
2008 *Hunting Art Prize Exhibition*, Houston
2008 *Invitational*, Lady Bird Johnson Wildflower Center, Austin
2009 Solo, Eugene Binder Exhibition Space, Marfa
2010 Solo, Museum of the Southwest, Midland
2010 Solo, Hunt Gallery, San Antonio
2011 Four-person show, San Angelo Museum of Fine Arts, San Angelo
2013 *Holidays at the Haley*, Haley Memorial Library & History Center, Midland
2014 *Invitational*, National Ranching Heritage Museum, Lubbock
2014–15 *Painting in the Texas Tradition*, traveled: Turner House, Dallas; Pearl Fincher Museum of Fine Arts, Spring (catalog)
2015 *Ties that Bind: Contemporary Texas Regionalism*, Turner House, Dallas
2015 *Texas Visions: Contemporary Texas Regionalism*, Nave Museum, Victoria
2015 *As Far as the Eye Can See: 100 Years of Texas Art*, Two Allen Center, Houston
2016 Solo, Hunt Gallery, San Antonio

SELECTED PUBLIC COLLECTIONS

Blue Bonnet Electric Cooperative, Bastrop
Data Foundry, Austin
Marfa National Bank, Marfa
McDonald Observatory, Fort Davis and Austin
Riata Energy, Dallas
Torch Energy Collection, Houston
University of Texas at San Antonio

David Caton (b. 1955, Pasadena, California)

David Caton is a painter whose work spans three decades of exploring landscape, still life, architectural, and mythological painting. Caton began to study painting during his high school years in Houston. He earned his BFA from the University of Houston and completed his MFA graduate studies at Yale University.

Throughout his early years, Caton exhibited regularly and was invited to be in group shows. He has since had numerous solo exhibitions, and his paintings are featured in corporate and private collections across the country.

Caton has a close affinity for the terrain of the west, especially that of the Big Bend region of Texas and the states of Utah and Arizona. He travels to these areas regularly to gather plein air painting material for future paintings. He usually executes studies in oil or pastel before completing the larger canvases. His refined technique and love for depicting the grandeur and drama that exist in nature have generated works that are both monumental and compelling.

SELECTED BIOGRAPHICAL AND CAREER HIGHLIGHTS

1974 *Houston Post* Scholastic Award, Museum of Fine Arts, Houston

1979 European Travel Grant, administered through the Museum of Fine Arts, Houston

1979 BFA, University of Houston

1980 Ford Foundation Graduate Assistance Grant, Yale University, New Haven, Connecticut

1981–82 Teaching Assistant to: Gretna Campbell (1981); Samia Halaby (1982)

1982 MFA, Yale University, New Haven, Connecticut

1985, 1987 National Endowment for the Arts Fellowship Grant

Resides in Utopia, Texas

SELECTED EXHIBITIONS

1975 *Annual Spring Exhibition*, Cullen Center, Houston

1975 *Truair, Hornbuckle, Sellers, and Caton*, One Allen Center, Houston

1977 *Houston Area Show*, Blaffer Gallery, University of Houston

1977 *Houston Invitational Painting*, Max Hutchinson Gallery, Houston

1979 Max Hutchinson Gallery, Houston

1979 *Miniature Show*, Lawndale Annex, University of Houston
1981 MSU Gallery, Texas A&M University, College Station
1982 Art and Architecture Gallery, Yale University, New Haven, Connecticut
1983 Group Show, Diverse Works, Houston
1984–86 Wilhelm Gallery, Houston
1986 *Lawndale Lab Show*, Lawndale Art Center, Houston
1987–88 Wilhelm Gallery, Scottsdale, Arizona
1987–88 Bienville Gallery, New Orleans, Louisiana
1988 *Houston '88*, Cullen Center, Houston
1988–90 Bell Ross Gallery, Memphis, Tennessee
1993 *Fur, Fins, Feathers and More: A Multi-Media Menagerie*, Galveston Art Center, Galveston
1994 *Romancing The Land*, Galveston Art Center, Galveston
1994 *Landscape Without Figures*, Hooks Epstein Gallery, Houston
1996 *Intimate, Houston Area Small Works Exhibition*, Davis Gallery/ Pennzoil Place Gallery, Houston
2001 *A Sense of Place,* Williams Tower, Houston
2001 Group Exhibition, Park Central VII, Dallas
2001 *Living and Working in Texas*, Park Central VII, VIII, and IX, Dallas
2001 *Still Lifes*, Transco Tower, Houston
2001 *David Caton & Libby Johnson*, Harris Gallery, Houston
2001 *Texas Landscapes*, Transco Tower, Houston
2001 Opening Exhibition, Barbara Able Gallery, Santa Fe, New Mexico
2002 Group Exhibition, Williams Tower, Houston
2002 Group Exhibition, Harris Gallery, Houston
2004 *David Caton and Bill Zaner*, Harris Gallery, Houston
2014 Solo, *The Contemporary Texas Visions of David Caton*, William Reaves Fine Art, Houston
2015 *Painting in the Texas Tradition*, Pearl Fincher Museum of Fine Arts, Spring (catalog)
2015 *Ties that Bind: Contemporary Regionalism*, Turner House, Dallas
2015 *Texas Visions: Contemporary Texas Regionalism*, Nave Museum, Victoria
2015 *As Far as the Eye Can See: 100 Years of Texas Art*, Two Allen Center, Houston

SELECTED PUBLIC COLLECTIONS

Houston: American General Corp., Andrews Kurth, Bank of America, Bank One, Chase Bank, Chevron, Dow Chemical, Duke Energy, Fidelity Investment, First City Bank, Hilton Americas, Houssiere, Durant & Doussiere, M. D. Anderson Hospital, Marathon Oil, Methodist Hospital, Northern Trust, Quanex, Schlumberger, Tenneco Inc., Transco Energy, Vinson & Elkins, Watt, Beckworth & Thompson, West University Bank

Other Texas Locations: Austin: Scott, Douglass & McConnico; College Station: Texas A&M University; Dallas: Electronic Data Systems, Heritage Media, Northern Trust, Societe Generale; Fort Worth: Omni American Credit Union; Midland: POGO; San Antonio: Chase Bank, USAA; The Woodlands: St. Luke's Hospital

Other States: AGL Resources, Atlanta, Georgia; Fidelity Investment, Denver, Colorado; Northwestern University Hospital, Chicago, Illinois; Sacred Heart Medical Center, Eugene, Oregon

Margie Crisp (b. 1960, New Orleans, Louisiana)

Originally from New Orleans, Margie Crisp resides in Elgin, just east of Austin, with her husband and fellow artist William Montgomery.

An award-winning author, Crisp divides her time between writing and creating art. Currently her primary mediums are egg tempera paintings on panel (often embellished with 24k gold leaf) and printmaking including linocuts and lithographs. She finds working in the traditional medium of egg tempera a meditative process and enjoys working with the dry pigments, mixing in egg yolk to produce the quick-drying and durable paint.

While birds are one of the primary subjects in her art, she does not consider herself a bird artist. She explains that birds are prevalent, abundant, and familiar. They inhabit the same spaces as people and are bold enough to confront them. She feels that the moment of communion between species compels her to repeatedly draw, paint, and print birds. Crisp describes her own work as grounded in reality: the particular, the focused, the well observed, or the specifically imagined.

SELECTED BIOGRAPHICAL AND CAREER HIGHLIGHTS

1984 Associate of Applied Science in Commercial Art/Advertising Design, with High Honors, Southwestern Technical College, Sylva, North Carolina

1991 BFA, with High Honors, University of Texas at Austin

2009 Writer in Residence, Thinking Like a Mountain Foundation, Fort Davis

2011 Artist in Residence, Madroño Ranch, Medina

2012 Authored *River of Contrasts: The Texas Colorado*, Texas A&M University Press

2012 Ron Tyler Award for Best Illustrated Book on Texas History and Culture, presented by Texas State Historical Association

2012 Carr P. Collins Award for Best Book of Non-Fiction, Texas Institute of Letters

Resides in Elgin, Texas

SELECTED EXHIBITIONS

1989 *Intimate Images: Small Works on Paper*, St. Edward's University, Austin

1995 *Counterpoint 1995*, Edd R. Turner Memorial Award, Hill Country Arts Foundation, Ingram

1995 *Art At Large: Billboard Art Competition*, one of three winners, Austin Visual Arts Association, Austin

1995 *Third Biennial Gulf of Mexico Symposium Juried Art Show*, Honorable Mention, Art Center of Corpus Christi

1996 *In the Garden: Katherine Brimberry and Margie Crisp*, Flatbed Press, Austin

1996 *Southwest '96*, Museum of New Mexico, Santa Fe, New Mexico

1997 *Contemporary Views: Images of Land and Nature*, Museum of the Big Bend, Alpine

1997 *New Lines, Women Printmakers of Austin*, St. Edward's University, Austin

1998 *Art School Faculty Exhibition*, Austin Museum of Art, Austin

1998 *National Works on Paper*, University of Texas at Tyler

2002 *People, Places and Things, Selections from the Permanent Collection*, Austin Museum of Art, Austin

2003 *North American Print Biennial*, Boston University, Boston, Massachusetts

2004 *Gardens, Real and Imagined*, Austin Museum of Art, Driscoll Villa, Austin

2005 *The Print Show*, Maryland Federation of Art City Gallery, Baltimore, Maryland

2007 *Migration*, A Gallery, Charlottesville, Virginia

2008 *Art, Science and the World Around Us*, Art Center of Waco

2011 *Perspective Influences Perception, Artwork from the Airport's Collection*, Phoenix Airport Museum, Phoenix

2011 *Fresh & Salty*, Fort Worth Community Arts Center, Fort Worth

2012 Solo, *River of Contrasts*: *Artwork of the Texas Colorado River by Margie Crisp*, Austin Bergstrom International Airport, Austin

2012 Solo, *River of Contrasts*: *The Texas Colorado*, Taste Wine & Art, Johnson City; Art Center of Waco

2012 *Contemporary Texas Regionalists*, traveled: Haley Memorial Library & History Center, Midland; Gage Hotel, Marathon

2012 Solo, *Tribute to a Texas River*: *Prints of the Colorado by Margie Crisp*, William Reaves Fine Art, Houston

2013 *Restless Heart*: *Contemporary Texas Regionalism*, San Angelo Museum of Fine Arts, San Angelo (catalog)

2013 *Celebrating the Regionalist Legacy in Texas Art*, William Reaves Fine Art and the San Angelo Museum of Fine Arts at the Gage Hotel, Marathon

2013 Solo, *Margie Crisp*: *Art of the Texas Colorado River*, Lady Bird Johnson Wildflower Center, Austin

2013 *Wings & Wheels, Artwork from the Airport's Collection*, Phoenix Airport Museum, Phoenix, Arizona

2013 *Holidays at the Haley*, Haley Memorial Library & History Center, Midland

2014–15 *Painting in the Texas Tradition*, traveled: Turner House, Dallas; Pearl Fincher Museum of Fine Arts, Spring (catalog)

2015 *Ties that Bind*: *Contemporary Texas Regionalism*, Turner House, Dallas

2015 *Texas Visions*: *Contemporary Texas Regionalism*, Nave Museum, Victoria

SELECTED PUBLIC COLLECTIONS

Art Museum of South Texas, Corpus Christi

Austin Museum of Art, Austin

Grace Museum, Abilene

Phoenix Arts Commission, Print Collection, Phoenix, Arizona

University of Texas at San Antonio

Tyler Museum of Art, Tyler

Keith Davis (b. 1955, Lubbock, Texas)

Keith Davis, a self-taught artist, began his love for producing art after a serious illness at the young age of nine. Walking down the corridors of the hospital, Davis was fascinated by the hanging oil portraits of doctors, amazed to see how a photorealistic image can be produced through paint. The young artist began to paint on his own.

Over time, Davis has developed his own style, finding inspiration in contemporary artists like David Bates and Jon Flaming, old masters including Pablo Picasso and Henri Matisse, and Texas regionalists such as Otis Dozier and Jerry Bywaters.

Davis collects subject matter from his daily life, often mixing in a little pop culture and quite a bit of imagination. His creative process begins with photos found on the Internet, especially the imagery with a folk art focus. For inspiration derived from his surroundings, Davis is continually drawn to the western Texas landscape of his youth and its spacious flatlands, stating that he loves how "free" it appears. He is also inspired by the beautiful hill country, especially in its parallel appearance and uniqueness relative to his native western flatlands.

The artist's oeuvre includes polychromed-wood sculptures that depict the various creatures that inhabit the Texas environment. For Davis, making art is a rewarding career and he continues to produce paintings and sculptures in his Austin studio.

SELECTED BIOGRAPHICAL AND CAREER HIGHLIGHTS

1974–76 South Plains Junior College, Levelland

2007–present Artist in Residence, Austin Visual Arts Association, Austin

2014 Finalist, Hunting Art Prize Competition

2014 Featured on the *Texas Country Reporter*

Resides in Austin, Texas

SELECTED EXHIBITIONS

2008 *Cowboy Love and a Bouquet of Flowers,* San Angelo Folk Art Gallery, San Antonio

2012 *Contemporary Texas Regionalists*, traveled: Haley Memorial Library & History Center, Midland; Gage Hotel, Marathon

2013 *Restless Heart: Contemporary Texas Regionalism,* San Angelo Museum of Fine Arts, San Angelo (catalog)

2013 *Celebrating the Regionalist Legacy in Texas Art,* William Reaves Fine Art and the San Angelo Museum of Fine Arts at the Gage Hotel, Marathon

2013 *Holidays at the Haley,* Haley Memorial Library & History Center, Midland

2014 *Hunting Art Prize Exhibition*, Houston

2014–15 *Painting in the Texas Tradition,* traveled: Turner House, Dallas; Pearl Fincher Museum of Fine Arts, Spring (catalog)

2015 *Ties that Bind: Contemporary Texas Regionalism*, Turner House, Dallas

2015 *Texas Visions: Contemporary Texas Regionalism*, Nave Museum, Victoria

SELECTED PUBLIC COLLECTIONS

Briscoe Museum of Western Art, San Antonio

Chevron Corporation, Corporate Headquarters, Midland

Fidencio Duran (b. 1961, Lockhart, Texas)

Fidencio Duran tells visual stories that honor the history of his family and community. These stories spring from recollections of his father's storytelling. "My dad used to tell us small parables about the consequences of being greedy or other moral lessons. He also wanted us to know where we came from, and all those old stories stuck with me."

Duran's artwork appears in public and private collections in the United States and abroad and his works have been exhibited by prestigious museums throughout the country. Duran has the distinction of being the only artist to receive all three Dallas Museum of Art Awards to Artists. One of his most prominent works, *The Visit*, graces the length of the ticket counter at Austin Bergstrom International Airport.

A recent series combines landscapes, nature, and found objects as metaphors for our human need for community and shelter. They espouse the value of living in close relation to the earth.

SELECTED BIOGRAPHICAL AND CAREER HIGHLIGHTS

1983 Clare Hart DeGolyer Memorial Fund Award, Dallas Museum of Art, Dallas

1984 Bachelor of Fine Arts (studio), University of Texas at Austin

1990 Arch M. Kimbrough Fund Award, Dallas Museum of Art, Dallas

1996 Dozier Travel Grant, Dallas Museum of Art, Dallas

2012 Artist in Residency Program Fellowship, Santa Fe Art Institute, Santa Fe, New Mexico

2015 Austin Arts Hall of Fame, Austin Critics Table, Austin

FEATURED IN:

"Good Mix, Visiones from Post Modern Aztlan," Roberta Fallon, *Philadelphia Weekly*, 2004

"More than Memories," Ben Bamsey, *Artworks*, Winter 2007

"Enmascarados," Alvaro Ibarra, *Fluent Collaborative*, December 2008

"Duran Pinta Historia Local," Liliana Valenzuela, *Ahora Si*, 2011

"Sunday Afternoon," Alexandra Landeros, *Latino Magazine*, Spring 2014

Resides in Austin, Texas

SELECTED EXHIBITIONS

1994 Solo, *Family/Community*: *Fidencio Duran*, Amarillo Art Museum, Amarillo

2005–07 Solo, *A Painted Memory*: *The Art of Fidencio Duran*, Nave Museum, Victoria; Grace Museum, Abilene; Mexic-Arte Museum, Austin; Chicago State University, Chicago, Illinois; Museo Latino, Omaha, Nebraska; Mesquite Art Center, Mesquite

2014 *Nuestras Historias*: *Stories of Mexican Identity from the Permanent Art Collection*, National Museum of Mexican Art, Chicago, Illinois

2014 Kenosha Public Museum, Kenosha, Wisconsin

2014 Shafer Gallery, Great Bend, Kansas

2014 Solo, *Tree of Life*, Gay Fay Kelly/Prizer Gallery, Austin

2015 John E. Conner Museum, Texas A&M University–Kingsville

2015 *Selections from the Contemporary Art Collection*, Mexic-Arte Museum, Austin

2016 *Estamos Aqui*, Crisp Museum, Southeast Missouri State University, Cape Girardeau, Missouri

2016 Oklahoma City Community College, Oklahoma City, Oklahoma

SELECTED PUBLIC COMMISSIONS

1996 Art in Public Places Program, *Comite Patriota, Diez y Seis, Cinco de Mayo*, Zaragoza Recreation Center, Austin

1999 Art in Public Places Program, *The Visit*, Austin Bergstrom International Airport, Austin

2000 South Texas Independent School District, *The Last Haven*, Biblioteca Las Americas, Mercedes

2004 University of Houston Permanent Collection, *Strength in Caring*, Center for Students with Disabilities, Houston

2011 El Centro, Austin Community College, *The Role and History of Education in East Austin Neighborhoods Govalle, Riverside, Montopolis, and Del Valle*, Riverside Campus, Austin

SELECTED PUBLIC COLLECTIONS

Art Museum of South Texas, Corpus Christi
Austin Contemporary, Austin
Grace Museum, Abilene
National Museum of Mexican Art, Chicago, Illinois
McNay Art Museum, San Antonio
Polk Museum of Art, Lakeland, Florida
San Angelo Museum of Fine Arts, San Angelo
San Antonio Museum of Art, San Antonio

Jon Flaming (b. 1962, Wichita, Kansas)

Jon Flaming is a multi-disciplined artist who is a designer, illustrator, and painter. His fine art focuses on small-town Texas and the Southwest. He is self-taught and works in a number of media, including watercolor, acrylic, oil, and found materials. Flaming's works clearly reflect the idiom of Texas regionalism and he has been classified as one of the state's foremost neo-regionalist painters. The art is done by a Texan for Texans, yet is still rich with universal narrative and appeal.

Flaming has tapped into an earlier regionalist sentiment and technique, evidenced by his iconic Texas subject matter. His paintings bring warm recollections of earlier, simpler roots, while simultaneously magnifying awareness of social change and transformation underway in the state of Texas.

He started Jon Flaming Design in 1993 and has created award-winning design campaigns and illustrations for a number of clients including Neiman Marcus, Milton Bradley, JC Penney, Pizza Hut, FedEx, Hewlett Packard, and Pepsi.

SELECTED BIOGRAPHICAL AND CAREER HIGHLIGHTS

1985 BFA, Texas State University, San Marcos

1993 Started Jon Flaming Design

Board of Directors, American Institute of Graphic Arts (AIGA)

Painting of Prince Albert Hunt selected for story by Christopher C. King in the Southern Music issue of the *Oxford American Magazine* 2014

Painting *House on a Hill* selected for cover of novel *Watt* by Samuel Beckett published by El Hilo de Ariadna, Argentina 2016

Resides in Richardson, Texas

SELECTED EXHIBITIONS

1995 Solo, Ken Knight Gallery, Dallas

1999 Solo, Texas State University, San Marcos

2004 Plano National Juried Show, Plano

2005 *Natural Disasters*, McKinney Avenue Contemporary, Dallas

2006, 2008 *Invitational*, Panhandle-Plains Historical Museum, Canyon

2006 Solo, Blue Star Gallery, Hico

2007 *Then and Now*, Texas State University, San Marcos

2007–08 *Cherry Spring Arts Festival*, Cherry Spring

2008 *Art in the Metroplex*, Texas Christian University, Fort Worth

2010 *Drawing on the Past: Selections from the Bobbie and John Nau Collection of Texas Art*, Grace Museum, Abilene

2010 *Nac Collect*, Cole Art Center, Nacogdoches

2011 *Texas Stampede*, Insight Gallery, Fredericksburg

2011 Solo, *Western Movie*, David Dike Fine Art, Dallas

2011, 2013 *Invitational*, Panhandle-Plains Historical Museum, Canyon

2012 *Contemporary Texas Regionalists*, traveled: Haley Memorial Library & History Center, Midland; Gage Hotel, Marathon

2013 *Restless Heart: Contemporary Texas Regionalism*, San Angelo Museum of Fine Arts, San Angelo (catalog)

2013 *Celebrating the Regionalist Legacy in Texas Art*, William Reaves Fine Art and the San Angelo Museum of Fine Arts at the Gage Hotel, Marathon

2013 Stephen F. Austin University, Nacogdoches
2013 Solo, *Birdston Valley Revival*, David Dike Fine Art, Dallas
2013 *Holidays at the Haley*, Haley Memorial Library & History Center, Midland
2014 *Painting in the Texas Tradition*, Turner House, Dallas
2014 Solo, *Oil on Canvas: Paintings of the Texas Oil & Gas Industry*, David Dike Fine Art, Dallas
2015 Solo, *McKinney*, Éclair Bistro, McKinney

SELECTED PUBLIC COLLECTIONS

Silver Eagle Distributors, Houston
Grace Museum, Abilene
San Angelo Museum of Fine Arts, San Angelo
Tyler Museum of Art, Tyler

Charles Ford (b. 1941, Dallas, Texas; d. 2016)

Charles Ford earned his bachelor of science degree in mechanical engineering from Lamar University and, for the next 15 years, worked in the field of engineering. In the early 1980s, he left for New York and had a successful career as a painter there for over nine years prior to returning to Texas.

As a photorealist painter, he strove to accurately convey the feeling of his environment through his vivid pieces. In his recent paintings of Houston, Ford captures the changing face of the Magnolia City, painting a wide range of subjects from iconic city landmarks, like the River Oaks Theater and the old Harold's Department Store, to scenes typically overlooked by the hurried passerby.

Through his meticulous attention to detail, Ford had a unique ability to single out moments and capture the character at the heart of his chosen locations. Each Texas scene exudes a true sense of place through his particular use of light, shadow, reflection, and color.

Just as in the work of Richard Estes and Chuck Close—forebears of the American photorealist movement of the late 1960s—Ford's paintings demonstrate the assimilation of photography into the art world. He typically works from color photographic stills to create paintings that appear to be photographs, almost mechanical in representation. Ford's efforts result in a series of consistently elegant renditions of the Texas scene, all characterized by exceptional composition and strong elements of color and light.

SELECTED BIOGRAPHICAL AND CAREER HIGHLIGHTS

1964 BS, Mechanical Engineering, Lamar University, Beaumont

Who's Who in American Art–1986, Jaques Cattell Press, 1986

Davenport's Art Reference: *The Gold Edition*, Ray Davenport, editor, Gordon's Art Reference, Inc., Phoenix, Arizona, 2005

The Artist's Bluebook: *34,000 North American Artists to March 2005*, edited by Lonnie Pierson Dunbier, AskART.com Inc., 2005

Died in Houston, Texas

SELECTED EXHIBITIONS

1979 *Dimension Houston*, Juried Exhibit, Art League of Houston, Houston

1979 Jewish Community Center of Houston, Juried Exhibit, Houston

1981 *New Artists at Madison Square Garden*, Juried Exhibit, New York

1982 Solo, Kaber Gallery, New York

1982 *The New Realists*, Cote Galleries, Rockville Center, Huntington, New York

1983 Prizewinner, *Beth-El Art Show*, Juried Exhibit, West Hartford, Connecticut

1984 Solo, Art Expo, New York

1984 Solo, The Uptown Gallery, New York

1984 *Painting New York*, Museum of the City of New York

1985 Two-person show, Las Vegas Museum of Contemporary Art, Las Vegas, Nevada

1985 Solo, Foxhall Gallery, Washington, DC

1986 *Urban Visions*, Uptown Gallery, New York

1986 Robinson Gallery, Los Angeles, California

1987 Gallery Henoch, New York

1988 Foxhall Gallery, Washington, DC

1988 ABC Show, Philadelphia, Pennsylvania

1989 Love Galleries, Chicago, Illinois

1989 *Works on Paper*, Queensborough Community Art Museum, New York

1990 *New Art from New York*, Juried Exhibit, traveled to Texas and California

1994 *Recent Acquisitions*, Museum of the City of New York

1999 Solo, Uptown Gallery, New York
2002 Solo, Williams Tower, Houston
2003 Two-person show, Harris Gallery, Houston
2004 *city_works*: *Recent Paintings*, Uptown Gallery, New York
2014 Solo, *Charles Ford*: *Texas Photorealism*, William Reaves Fine Art, Houston
2015 *Painting in the Texas Tradition*, Pearl Fincher Museum of Fine Arts, Spring (catalog)
2015 *Ties that Bind*: *Contemporary Texas Regionalism*, Turner House, Dallas
2015 *Texas Visions*: *Contemporary Texas Regionalism*, Nave Museum, Victoria

SELECTED PUBLIC COLLECTIONS

Chevron Corporation, Corporate Headquarters, Midland
Columbia Pictures, Private and Corporate Collections, California
Gruntal Corporation, New York
Museum of the City of New York
Trump Castle Hotel, Atlantic City, New Jersey
Zabar's, New York

Pat Gabriel (b. 1960, Chicago, Illinois)

Pat Gabriel began drawing and sculpting as a child but became much more serious about producing art during his teenage years. At age fourteen, he met Yan Macs, a Latvian-born painter, and re-established his inspirational compass. He began working with acrylic paints and producing highly detailed paintings. After he graduated, Gabriel immediately began working as a commercial artist and started moving his way up in the advertising field. Although the commitments of his daily life limited his time, the direction and quality of Gabriel's work matured over time, and he later began working with oils and studying mainly European artists.

Gabriel is greatly inspired by clouds and what they do to light; he often paints the transformation of light and color frequently seen in the Texas landscape. In addition, he draws inspiration from plant life and keeps an elaborate garden. Working slowly, Gabriel spends quite a bit of time considering what to paint and says that many of his paintings are symbolic or perhaps allegorical. Highlighting the collision of nature and man-made elements, he creates figurative painting through landscape imagery.

In most cases, Gabriel begins with small idea sketches, working on many ideas at once. He photographs subjects of interest and then edits the images to create a final painting reference. His greatest aspiration is to make the viewer experience the same feelings he had while he was painting. Bringing the awe he experienced when he noticed the shifts of light in the morning sky to his pieces, Gabriel conveys ideas that are personal to him but are universal to his audiences.

SELECTED BIOGRAPHICAL AND CAREER HIGHLIGHTS

1966 Moved to Fort Worth, Texas

1990–present Executive Director of Creative Services at GCG Marketing, Fort Worth

2009 Gail and Bill Landreth Award in memory of Gene Owens, *Preservation is the Art of the City*, Fort Worth Community Arts Center, Fort Worth

2011 Lucy Brants and Harry Brants Award in memory of Cynthia Brants, *Preservation is the Art of the City*, Fort Worth Community Arts Center, Fort Worth

2011 Hunting Art Prize Poster, Painting *Fragile Spring* selected for poster image

Advisory Panel Member, Fort Worth Community Arts Center

Show previewed by Bonnie Gangelhoff, *Southwest Art Magazine*, Vol. 44, No. 10, March 2015

Resides in Fort Worth, Texas

SELECTED EXHIBITIONS

2007 *The 9×12 Works on Paper Show*, Fort Worth Community Arts Center, Fort Worth

2008 *Fort Worth Community Arts Center 2008 Biennial*, Fort Worth

2008 *Advisory Panel Selects*, Fort Worth Community Arts Center, Fort Worth

2009 *Texas Artists Coalition Juried Membership Show*, Fort Worth Community Arts Center, Fort Worth

2009–11 *Preservation is the Art of the City*, Fort Worth Community Arts Center, Fort Worth

2010–11 *Hunting Art Prize Exhibition*, Houston

2011 *Contemporaries: A Survey of 21st Century American Artists*, Central Library, Fort Worth

2012 *Contemporary Texas Regionalists*, traveled: Haley Memorial Library & History Center, Midland; Gage Hotel, Marathon

2013 *Restless Heart: Contemporary Texas Regionalism*, San Angelo Museum of Fine Arts, San Angelo (catalog)

2013 *Celebrating the Regionalist Legacy in Texas Art*, William Reaves Fine Art and the San Angelo Museum of Fine Arts at the Gage Hotel, Marathon

2013 *Holidays at the Haley*, Haley Memorial Library & History Center, Midland

2014 *Hunting Art Prize Exhibition*, Houston

2014–15 *Painting in the Texas Tradition*, traveled: Turner House, Dallas; Pearl Fincher Museum of Fine Arts, Spring (catalog)

2015 *Ties that Bind: Contemporary Texas Regionalism*, Turner House, Dallas

2015 Solo, *Pat Gabriel: In Plain Sight*, William Reaves Fine Art, Houston

2015 *Texas Visions: Contemporary Texas Regionalism*, Nave Museum, Victoria

2015 *The Real Show*, Old Jail Art Center, Albany

2015 *As Far as the Eye Can See: 100 Years of Texas Art*, Two Allen Center, Houston

SELECTED PUBLIC COLLECTIONS

BNSF Railroad Collection, Fort Worth

Chevron Corporation, Corporate Headquarters, Midland

Gage Hotel, Marathon

GCG Marketing, Fort Worth

Hunter George (b. 1932, Lynchburg, Virginia)

Hunter George studied art, design, and photography at Virginia Commonwealth University in Richmond where he earned a bachelor of fine arts degree.

As a graphic artist from 1960–2000, he was honored with numerous design awards from Art Directors' Clubs of New York, Los Angeles, Denver, Tulsa, and Houston; Communication Arts Magazine; Print Magazine; Ad Week Magazine; The Printing Industries of America; and the Dallas, Fort Worth Society of Communication Arts. He is a past president of the Art Directors' Club of Houston and has served on the Texas State Board of the American Institute of Graphic Artists.

Hunter George has always hungered to capture the natural as well as the historical in watercolor. He would like to help preserve a cultural history that is quickly fading from our midst. His love of old buildings and landscapes dominates his portfolio called "Reflections of the Past."

Since becoming a full-time watercolorist in 2000, Hunter's prize-winning paintings have been featured in art galleries throughout the state of Texas. A longtime member of the Watercolor Art Society of Houston, Hunter has had paintings accepted in the Houston International Watercolor Shows for five years, granting him Signature status in the society. His award-winning works have also been showcased in *Texas Highways Magazine* and at the Lady Bird Johnson Wildflower Center in Austin.

SELECTED BIOGRAPHICAL AND CAREER HIGHLIGHTS

1952 Korean War Veteran, United States Air Force
1959 BFA, Virginia Commonwealth University, Richmond, Virginia
1960–75 Graphic Designer and Art Director, Houston
1975–85 Partner, Advertising Agency, Houston
1985–2000 President, Hunter George Graphic Design, Houston
1986 Board Member, American Institute of Graphic Artists (AIGA)
2000–present Watercolors by Hunter, Houston
Signature Membership, Watercolor Art Society-Houston (WAS-H)
Member: Rockport Society for the Arts; Arts for Rural Texas; Center for the Advancement and Study of Early Texas Art (CASETA)
2008 Honorable Mention, *Annual International Show*, Watercolor Art Society-Houston (WAS-H)
Resides in Houston, Texas

SELECTED EXHIBITIONS

Blair House Gallery, Wimberly
Hunt Gallery, San Antonio
Simply Art Gallery, Galveston
Creekside Gallery, Belton
Holland House Gallery, Bellville
Griffith Gallery, Salado

Lady Bird Johnson Wildflower Center, Austin
Texas Highways Magazine, Austin
2006–08 *Annual International Show*, Watercolor Art Society-Houston (WAS-H)
2010, 2012 *Annual International Show*, Watercolor Art Society-Houston (WAS-H)

SELECTED PUBLIC COLLECTIONS

Cultural Activities Center, Temple
Texas Oil Museum, Luling

Billy Hassell (b. 1956, Dallas, Texas)

Fort Worth–based fine artist Billy Hassell, who was recently referred to as "Mother Nature's Stylist" by *The New York Times*, has been showing his artwork since the 1980s in galleries across the country. His bold colors and patterns inspired by nature have captured the imagination of collectors throughout the nation. Few artists use color as effectively as Hassell, and his graphically illustrative style contributes to his work's emotional punch.

Elite museums in Texas such as the Dallas Museum of Art, the Modern in Fort Worth, the Houston Museum of Fine Arts, and the Menil Collection in Houston, among others, have acquired Hassell's oil paintings for their permanent collections. His works also hang in many other public art collections including a US Embassy, the University of Texas, the offices of HBO, and the George W. Bush Presidential Center.

National art magazines such as *Art News*, *Southwest Art*, *The New York Times*, and the *Wall Street Journal* have featured Hassell's paintings as well as many regional publications including the *Dallas Morning News*, the *Houston Chronicle*, the *Fort Worth Star-Telegram*, *D magazine*, and *360 West*. His artwork has also been displayed on several television shows. Because of his dedication to conservation, Hassell has donated art throughout his career to conservation organizations. The Nature Conservancy, Ocean Conservation, and Audubon have used his artwork to raise money for environmental causes and celebrate the beauty of nature.

A unique passion is printmaking—in particular, lithographs. Hassell has collaborated with a number of master printers to produce a sizeable number of color lithographs. This increasingly rare and labor-intensive form of printmaking has been, and continues to be, sought after by collectors internationally.

His talents are not limited to the canvas. Hassell has produced and designed large-scale stained-glass murals, one of which is a large floor medallion for the Dallas/Fort Worth Airport; another, a 50-foot mural at a fire station in Fort Worth. He has also worked on various public art projects.

Academia has been an ongoing interest throughout his life. Hassell earned his BFA from Notre Dame, followed by his MFA from the University of Massachusetts in Amherst. Upon completion of his graduate degree, Notre Dame invited him back as a professor to teach etching and watercolor. He has also taught a variety of art classes—painting, drawing, printmaking, and studio practices—at universities including Davidson College in North Carolina.

Hassell is regularly invited to people's ranches and other landscapes across the country, as well as out of the country, to capture the unique beauty of private places for their owners. Most recently, he completed a mural at a ranch in the Texas Hill Country that was featured in the *Wall Street Journal*.

Today, Hassell's work continues to show the natural world charged with life, energy, and movement. On canvases that loom larger than life, both in size and vibrancy of subject, his distinctive use of color and stylized natural elements and animals reveal why he has become such a highly-respected painter.

SELECTED BIOGRAPHICAL AND CAREER HIGHLIGHTS

1981 Best in Show, *New England Artist Festival & Showcase*, NEAF Gallery, Northampton, Massachusetts

1982 BFA, University of Notre Dame, South Bend, Indiana

1987 MFA, University of Massachusetts, Amherst, Massachusetts

1984 Award, *19th Annual Juried Art Exhibition*, Jewish Community Center, Houston

1984 Award, *Competition '84*, Assistance League, Two Houston Center, Houston
1984 Best of Series, *Emerging Artists, 1984*; Galveston Arts Center, Galveston
1984 Cover of the 1984 Houston Arts Calendar & Directory, Houston
1985 Anne Giles Kimbrough Award, Dallas Museum of Art, Dallas
1989 Honorable Mention, *31st Annual Invitational Exhibition*, Longview Museum of Fine Arts, Longview
2002 Best of Show, *42nd Annual Invitational Exhibition*, Longview Museum of Fine Arts, Longview
Resides in Fort Worth, Texas

SELECTED EXHIBITIONS

1980 *Alumni/Faculty Exhibition*, Snite Museum of Art, University of Notre Dame, South Bend, Indiana
1980 *Boston Community Art Exhibition*, Boston City Hall, Boston, Massachusetts
1980 *Drawing Exhibition*, University of Massachusetts, Amherst
1980 Juried Exhibition, Edison Community College, Fort Meyers, Florida
1981 *Four Painters*, University of Massachusetts, Amherst
1982 Thesis Exhibition, Herter Gallery, University of Massachusetts, Amherst
1982 *Works on Paper*, University of Massachusetts, Amherst
1983 *Maps: A Mail Art Show*, Diverse Works, Inc., Houston
1983 *Synergy '83*, Glassell School of Art, Houston
1984 *19th Annual Juried Art Award Exhibition*, Jewish Community Center, Houston
1984 *Artist Call*, Lawndale Annex, University of Houston
1984 *Competition '84*, Two Houston Center, Houston
1984 *Four Texas Artists*, Galveston Arts Center, Galveston
1984 *Houston Profile*, Art League of Houston
1984 *Texas Only*, Laguna Gloria Museum, Austin
1985 *East End Show*, Lawndale Annex, University of Houston
1985 Solo, Galveston Arts Center, Galveston
1985 *Propaganda*, Midtown Art Center, Houston
1985 *Self-Image*, Midtown Art Center, Houston
1985 *Southwest '85*, Museum of Fine Arts, Santa Fe, New Mexico

1985 *Texas Visions*, Transco Tower, Houston
1986 *Faculty Exhibition*, Snite Museum of Art, University of Notre Dame, South Bend, Indiana
1987 Solo, University of Arizona, Tucson, Arizona
1988 *American Artists' Beastiary*: *Armadillo to Zebra*, Amarillo Art Center, Amarillo
1989 *31st Annual Invitational Exhibition*, Longview Museum of Fine Arts, Longview
1989 Solo, Davidson College Art Gallery, Davidson, North Carolina
1989 *Feather, Fur & Fin*, Laguna Gloria Museum, Austin
1989 *Print Makers*, Aquinas College, Grand Rapids, Michigan
1989 *The Nature of the Beast*, Hudson River Museum, Westchester, New York
1990 *Forty Texas Printmakers*, Modern Art Museum of Fort Worth
1991 *Chords and Discords*, Hudson River Museum, Westchester, New York
1992 *100 Anniversary Exhibition*: *Masterworks from Fort Worth Collections*, Modern Art Museum of Fort Worth
1992 *Printmaking in Texas*: *The 1980s*, Laguna Gloria Museum, Austin
1992 *The Big Show*, Lawndale Art Center, Houston
1992–95 *Contemporary Prints*: *The Peregrine Press Archives*, traveling exhibit
1993 *Animal Attraction*, University of Dallas Art Gallery, Dallas
1993 *Art and the Animals*, Longview Museum of Fine Arts, Longview
1993 *Talleres en Fronteras*: *An Exhibition of Contemporary Art from South Texas and Baja California*, Corpus Christi State University, Corpus Christi, traveling exhibit
1993 *Texas Art Celebration '93*, Cullen Center, Houston
1993 *Texas Select Invitational Exhibition*, Wichita Falls Museum and Art Center, Wichita Falls
1994 *All Creatures Great and Small*, Dallas Museum of Art, Dallas
1994 *Collector's Choice*: *Living with Art*, Laguna Gloria Museum, Austin
1995 *Texas Myths and Realities*, Museum of Fine Arts, Houston
1998 *Texas Roots*, Center for the Visual Arts, Denton
2001 *Faculty Biennial Exhibition*, University of Texas at Arlington
2001 *Made in Texas*, Art Center of Waco
2002 *42nd Annual Invitational Exhibition*, Longview Museum of Fine Arts, Longview

2002 Solo, Longview Museum of Fine Arts, Longview
2003 *Art in the Metroplex*, Texas Christian University, Fort Worth
2003 *For the Birds*, Galveston Arts Center, Galveston
2006 *Blurring Boundaries*, Ellen Noel Art Museum, Odessa
2007 *Margarita Cabrera and Billy Hassell*, The Gallery, University of Texas at Arlington
2007–09 Solo, *Migration, 15 Year Survey*, Art Museum of South Texas, Corpus Christi; Texas A&M International University, Laredo; Ellen Noel Museum of Art, Odessa
2008 *Art, Science and the World Around Us*, Art Center of Waco
2008 *Public Art in Fort Worth*, Forth Worth Public Library, Fort Worth
2010 *Advancing Tradition: 25 Years of Printmaking at Flatbed Press*, Austin Museum of Art, Austin
2010 Solo, *Memento*, Mabee-Gerrer Museum of Art, Shawnee, Oklahoma
2010 *Collections, Cultures & Collaborations*, University of North Texas, Denton
2012 *Wild Things* (with David Everett), Grace Museum, Abilene
2013 Solo, *Illuminating Nature*, Tyler Museum of Art, Tyler
2014 Solo, *Ephemera: Winged Creatures of Texas*, Botanical Research Institute of Texas (BRIT), Fort Worth
2015 *Painting in the Texas Tradition*, Pearl Fincher Museum of Fine Arts, Spring (catalog)
2015 *Ties that Bind: Contemporary Texas Regionalism*, Turner House, Dallas
2015 *Texas Visions: Contemporary Texas Regionalism*, Nave Museum, Victoria
2015 *As Far as the Eye Can See: 100 Years of Texas Art*, Two Allen Center, Houston

SELECTED PUBLIC COMMISSIONS

1982 University of Massachusetts, Fine Arts Center Auditorium, Amherst, two murals
1991 Methodist Medical Center, Dallas, oil on canvas
1991–92 Cistercian Abbey, Irving, Tabernacle door (bronze)
1992 Home Box Office (HBO), Dallas, oil on canvas
1992 Texas Nature Conservancy, San Antonio, color intaglio edition
1995 VHA, Inc., Dallas, two oils on canvas
2002 University of Texas at Austin, A.C.E.S. Building, Austin, oil on canvas

2002–05 Dallas/Fort Worth International Airport, Terminal D, design for mosaic floor medallion, *Early Morning Flight*

2002–07 Audubon Society of Texas, Austin, five limited-edition color lithographs

2007–08 Fire Station #34, Sendera Ranch, Fort Worth, design/implementation of exterior mosaic

2015–18 Texas Parks and Wildlife Foundation, Austin, *Keeping it Wild Campaign*, five limited-edition color lithographs

SELECTED PUBLIC COLLECTIONS

Dallas–Fort Worth Metroplex: Irving; Crescent Collection, Dallas; Dallas Museum of Art, Dallas; Frito-Lay, Inc., Department of Research and Development, Plano; George W. Bush Presidential Center, Southern Methodist University, Dallas; Modern Art Museum of Fort Worth; Texas Instruments, Dallas

Other Texas Locations: Art Museum of South Texas, Corpus Christi; Chevron Corporation, Corporate Headquarters, Midland; Ellen Noel Museum of Art, Odessa; Longview Museum of Fine Arts, Longview; Menil Collection, Houston; Museum of Fine Arts, Houston; Tyler Museum of Art, Tyler; Wichita Falls Museum and Art Center, Wichita Falls

Mexico: US Consulate General, Ciudad Juarez, Mexico

Lee Jamison (b. 1957, Shreveport, Louisiana)

As a very young child, Lee Jamison developed an interest for art. He started drawing as soon as he could hold something to make a mark with. He recalls beginning to paint around eight years of age, and he was constantly involved in art classes through high school. He chose to major in art at Lon Morris College, a small Methodist junior college in Jacksonville, Texas, and completed his degree at Centenary College in Shreveport, Louisiana.

Jamison feels that drawing is a form of expression, similar to writing, and he simply expresses things he knows through his art. He enjoys working in series that are often rich with historical influence. While he has no set process for creating a work, he describes his paintings as ideas vaguely bubbling up from below. His historical works always begin with a recorded event, but the potential connection of historical occurrences to modern-day issues drive him to create pieces compelling to the viewer. Essentially, Jamison's artwork is his own historical exploration.

Since 1982, Jamison has been a full-time artist. He is known for three major specialties: landscapes in oils (particularly of East and Central Texas), large murals, and historical paintings. His landscapes have been the mainstay of a career spanning a quarter of a century. His mural projects have included major works for the Driskill Hotel in Austin and the University of Texas at Austin. His historical works draw on his knowledge of Texas history and include numerous works on the Texas revolution.

SELECTED BIOGRAPHICAL AND CAREER HIGHLIGHTS

1977 AA, Art, Lon Morris College, Jacksonville, Texas

1979 BA, Art, Centenary College of Louisiana, Shreveport, Louisiana

2011 The Sam Houston Project, produced nine credited works for combination documentary film and website on the life of Sam Houston

Resides in Huntsville, Texas

SELECTED EXHIBITIONS

2012 *Contemporary Texas Regionalists*, traveled: Haley Memorial Library & History Center, Midland; Gage Hotel, Marathon

2013 *Restless Heart: Contemporary Texas Regionalism*, San Angelo Museum of Fine Arts, San Angelo (catalog)

2013 *Celebrating the Regionalist Legacy in Texas Art*, William Reaves Fine Art and the San Angelo Museum of Fine Arts at the Gage Hotel, Marathon

2013 *Holidays at the Haley*, Haley Memorial Library & History Center, Midland

2014–15 *Painting in the Texas Tradition*, traveled: Turner House, Dallas; Pearl Fincher Museum of Fine Arts, Spring (catalog)

2015 *Ties that Bind: Contemporary Texas Regionalism*, Turner House, Dallas

2015 *Texas Visions: Contemporary Texas Regionalism*, Nave Museum, Victoria

SELECTED PUBLIC COLLECTIONS

Bastrop County History Mural, Bastrop

Driskill Hotel Ballroom, Austin
Elgin Community Mural, Elgin
Kellogg-Pritchett House, Huntsville
Mayborn Museum Complex, (numerous murals and dioramas, significant work on installation of the museum, and work on development of the Emergence of Man Gallery), Baylor University, Waco
Scott E. Johnson Memorial Mural, Huntsville
Texas Memorial Stadium, University of Texas at Austin
Waco Mammoth Site Murals, Waco
Walker County Storm Shelter Mural, Huntsville
Bastrop County Historical Association Museum, Bastrop
Lon Morris College, Jacksonville

Robb Kendrick (b. 1963, Spur, Texas)

Robb Kendrick has been interested in photography from a young age. He grew into a self-taught photographer and chose photography as his major in college. Kendrick says that he is inspired by people and the environments that shape their lives. His work is greatly influenced by the Texas characteristics of independence and pride as well as the rough environment and challenging weather.

Over the years, Robb Kendrick's photos for *National Geographic* have won him international recognition. In the past decade, however, his work as a tintype artist has earned him even wider acclaim. Kendrick has resurrected the tintype format, a photo technique from the mid-19th century, to bring a haunting timelessness to his portrait subjects, which include cowboys from the West, Tarahumara Indians in Northern Mexico, and mummies in Guanajuato, Mexico. The tintype photos he creates with the wet-plate process are all handmade from start to finish, making each a unique, one-of-a-kind image.

Kendrick has published four books of tintypes. His first book, *Revealing Character: Texas Tintypes*, was also a traveling exhibition featured at eight major museums throughout Texas. The wet-plate portraits of working cowboys in *Still: Cowboys at the Start of the 21st Century* were made in fourteen Western states, Mexico, and Canada.

Kendrick believes that his art is driven by connecting with people, sharing stories and meals together, and capturing them in their environments.

SELECTED BIOGRAPHICAL AND CAREER HIGHLIGHTS

1981–85 East Texas State University, Commerce

Frequent Instructor for National Geographic seminars and workshops

Author of:

Revealing Character: Texas Tintypes, Bright Sky Press, 2005

Still: Cowboys at the Start of the 21st Century, University of Texas Press, 2008

Changelings, Cloverleaf Press, 2009

History of the Waggoner Ranch, Four-O Publishing, 2011

Images published in:

In Focus: National Geographic Greatest Portraits, cover image, November 2004

"21st Century Cowboys," *National Geographic*, December 2007

Resides in Austin, Texas

SELECTED EXHIBITIONS

2004 *Best Portraits of National Geographic*, Smithsonian Institution, Washington, DC

2005–07 Solo exhibition of tintypes, Art Museum of South Texas, Corpus Christi; Bob Bullock Texas State History Museum, Austin; International Museum of Art and Science, McAllen; National Cowgirl Museum, Fort Worth; Old Jail Art Center, Albany; Panhandle-Plains Historical Museum, Canyon; Ranching Heritage Center, Lubbock; Witte Museum, San Antonio

2011 Solo retrospective, *The Wittliff Collections*, Texas State University, San Marcos

2012 *Contemporary Texas Regionalists*, traveled: Haley Memorial Library & History Center, Midland; Gage Hotel, Marathon

2012 Solo, *The Cowboy Spirit: Faces of the American West by Robb Kendrick*, William Reaves Fine Art, Houston

2013 *Restless Heart: Contemporary Texas Regionalism*, San Angelo Museum of Fine Arts, San Angelo (catalog)

2013 *Celebrating the Regionalist Legacy in Texas Art*, William Reaves Fine Art and the San Angelo Museum of Fine Arts at the Gage Hotel, Marathon

2013 *Holidays at the Haley*, Haley Memorial Library & History Center, Midland

2014–15 *Painting in the Texas Tradition*, traveled: Turner House, Dallas; Pearl Fincher Museum of Fine Arts, Spring (catalog)

2015 *Ties that Bind: Contemporary Texas Regionalism*, Turner House, Dallas

2015 *Texas Visions: Contemporary Texas Regionalism*, Nave Museum, Victoria

SELECTED PUBLIC COLLECTIONS

Frost Bank, San Antonio

Harry Ransom Center, the University of Texas at Austin

Icon Bank, Houston

Museum of Fine Arts, Houston

Ralph Lauren Collections

Rockwell Museum, Corning, New York

Wittliff Collections, Texas State University, San Marcos

Laura Lewis (b. 1954, Austin, Texas)

Laura Lewis quickly noticed her interest in art when a self-portrait assignment in the third grade depicted her gift for drawing. Pursuing artistic education throughout her adolescence, Lewis was fortunate to study portraiture under renowned artist Glenna Goodacre.

At the beginning of her college years, Lewis majored in art but later changed her field of study to health sciences. She graduated with a degree in the health sciences and had a long career in the medical field. However, throughout her years as a medical employee, her artistic passion did not disappear, and Lewis continued to paint portraits, learn print making techniques, and study with accomplished artists such as Paul Milosevich and Carroll Collier. Lewis has been a full-time professional artist since 2001 and continues to study through workshops with artists such as George Strickland, Matt Smith, and Camille Przwodek.

Lewis states that portraying the rugged beauty of the High Plains of Texas is her most gratifying challenge. She focuses her artistic gift on successfully conveying the grandeur of the Texas landscape to her audiences.

SELECTED BIOGRAPHICAL AND CAREER HIGHLIGHTS

1978 BS, Southwest Texas State University, San Marcos

2001–present Regionalist Painter of the High Plains of Texas

2004 Best of Show, *Red River Valley National Juried Show*, Vernon

2012 Best of Show, *Lubbock Art Festival Juried Exhibit*, Lubbock

2013 First Place, *Lubbock Art Festival Juried Exhibit*, Lubbock

Articles authored or referenced in:

"Using Rhythm and Movement to Create Harmonious Landscapes" by Jana Fowler, *American Artist Magazine*, February 2009

"Landscapes Reimagined" by Mary Lance, *Texas Co-op Power Magazine*, July 2010

"The Complete Painter's Handbook" published by *American Artist Magazine,* 2012

"Advice for Sustaining an Artistic Career," American Artist Workshop (a special issue of *American Artist Magazine*) 2012

"Build Audiences with E-Portfolios" by E. Brady Robinson, *Professional Artist Magazine*, October/November 2014

2016 Mural commissioned by Chevron Corporation for Corporate Headquarters, Midland, Texas (*100 Years in Oil)*

Resides in Mason, Texas

SELECTED EXHIBITIONS

2000 Pastel Society of New Mexico, Fisher Gallery, Albuquerque, New Mexico

2004 *Midland Arts Association National Juried Show*, Museum of the Southwest, Midland

2004–05 *Red River Valley National Juried Show*, Vernon

2005 Solo, *Rhythm in the Landscape*, Louise Hopkins Underwood Center for the Arts, Lubbock

2007 Solo, *West Texas Landscapes*, McCormick Gallery, Midland

2007 *The Big Picture*, EdibleMetal Gallery, Lubbock

2008 *Lubbock Centennial Celebration*: *50 Years of Art*, Louise Hopkins Underwood Center for the Arts, Lubbock

2009, 2011 Solo, Art on Texas Avenue, Lubbock

2010 Solo, Weiler House Fine Art, Fort Worth

2011 Southwest Gallery, Dallas

2012–13 *Lubbock Art Festival Juried Exhibit*, Louise Hopkins Underwood Center for the Arts, Lubbock

2012 *Contemporary Texas Regionalists*, traveled: Haley Memorial Library & History Center, Midland; Gage Hotel, Marathon

2013 *Restless Heart: Contemporary Texas Regionalism*, San Angelo Museum of Fine Arts, San Angelo (catalog)

2013 *Celebrating the Regionalist Legacy in Texas Art*, William Reaves Fine Art and the San Angelo Museum of Fine Arts at the Gage Hotel, Marathon

2013 Solo, *About Place: Paintings of Laura Lewis*, Louise Hopkins Underwood Center for the Arts, Lubbock

2013 *Holidays at the Haley*, Haley Memorial Library & History Center, Midland

2014–15 *Painting in the Texas Tradition*, traveled: Turner House, Dallas; Pearl Fincher Museum of Fine Arts, Spring (catalog)

2015 *Ties that Bind: Contemporary Texas Regionalism*, Turner House, Dallas

2015 *Texas Visions: Contemporary Texas Regionalism*, Nave Museum, Victoria

2015 *As Far as the Eye Can See: 100 Years of Texas Art*, Two Allen Center, Houston

SELECTED PUBLIC COLLECTIONS

ARMTech Insurance Services, Lubbock
Benchmark Business Solutions, Lubbock
Chevron Corporation, Midland
Chromatin, Inc., Lubbock
First United Bank, Lubbock
Glasheen Valles Inderman LLP, Lubbock
Happy State Bank, Amarillo
Plains Cotton Cooperative Association, Lubbock
San Angelo Museum of Fine Arts, San Angelo
WindTex Energy LP, Dallas

William Montgomery (b. 1953, Tyler, Texas)

William Montgomery is a painter and printmaker who lives near Elgin, just east of Austin. Growing up in Tyler, he studied art at the Kansas City

Art Institute and the University of New Mexico. While studying at the Academia de Belle Arti de Perugia in Italy, Montgomery developed an interest in classical European painting that had a major influence on his painting technique as well as his approach to subject matter. A life long fascination with nature is a continuing influence and his current work explores animals in their environments, particularly their convergence with civilization.

Montgomery is also an accomplished printmaker. His twin interests in natural history and traditional etching techniques contribute to skilled and sometimes humorous prints, mainly of Texas and its residents. His scientifically precise etchings of snakes have appeared on the covers of a number of important herpetology books.

Montgomery is currently working on a series of paintings about the Nueces River of Texas that will be part of a book he is collaborating on with his wife, author and artist Margie Crisp.

SELECTED BIOGRAPHICAL AND CAREER HIGHLIGHTS

1972 TFAA Scholarship, Texas Fine Arts Association

1973–74 University of New Mexico, Albuquerque, New Mexico

1974 Perugia Fine Arts Academy, Perugia, Italy

1974–75 Kansas City Art Institute, Kansas City, Missouri

1975–77 University of New Mexico, Albuquerque, New Mexico

1996 Award of Merit, *Southwest '96*, Museum of New Mexico, Santa Fe, New Mexico

Resides in Elgin, Texas

SELECTED EXHIBITIONS

1976 *Two Edges on a Line*, ASA Gallery, Albuquerque, New Mexico

1977 Solo, *William B. Montgomery*, Triple G Gallery, Providence, Rhode Island

1979 *New Works—Carol Ivey and William B. Montgomery*, Laguna Gloria Museum, Austin

1979 *National Print Invitational*, University of Dallas (touring)

1983 *New Figurative Drawing in Texas*, San Antonio Art Institute Gallery, San Antonio

1983 *Four State Survey*, Santa Fe Festival of the Arts, Santa Fe, New Mexico

1985 *Southwest '85*, Museum of Santa Fe, New Mexico

1985 *26th Annual Invitational Exhibition*, Longview Museum of Fine Arts, Longview

1988 Solo, *William Montgomery, Recent Works*, Tyler Museum of Art, Tyler

1992 *20th Anniversary Exhibition, 1972–1992*, Art Center of Waco

1996 *Southwest '96*, Museum of New Mexico, Santa Fe

2008 *Art, Science and the World Around Us*, Art Center of Waco

2009 Solo, *Nature Under Pressure: Etchings and Lithographs by William B. Montgomery*, Tyler Museum of Art, Tyler

2012 *Contemporary Texas Regionalists*, traveled: Haley Memorial Library & History Center, Midland; Gage Hotel, Marathon

2013 *Restless Heart: Contemporary Texas Regionalism*, San Angelo Museum of Fine Arts, San Angelo (catalog)

2013 *Celebrating the Regionalist Legacy in Texas Art*, William Reaves Fine Art and the San Angelo Museum of Fine Arts at the Gage Hotel, Marathon

2013 *Holidays at the Haley*, Haley Memorial Library & History Center, Midland

2014–15 *Painting in the Texas Tradition*, traveled: Turner House, Dallas; Pearl Fincher Museum of Fine Arts, Spring (catalog)

2015 *Ties that Bind: Contemporary Texas Regionalism*, Turner House, Dallas

2015 *Texas Visions: Contemporary Texas Regionalism*, Nave Museum, Victoria

SELECTED PUBLIC COLLECTIONS

Art Center of Waco

Dallas Museum of Art, Dallas

Tyler Museum of Art, Tyler

Noe Perez (b. 1958, Falfurrias, Texas)

Interested in art from a young age, Perez's artistic education began in his early teens as he studied with various local artists. Despite his love of art, he chose to major in engineering. Perez earned his bachelor of science degree in civil engineering at A&I University, and he continues to work in that field today.

Unwilling to put aside his intense interest in art, Perez has continued to advance his artistic abilities, attending plein air painting workshops with Plein-Air Painters of America artists Ron Rencher and George Strickland. Much of his work is done in the studio from photographs and plein air studies.

Perez believes that plein air painting is an essential exercise for any landscape painter and he paints outdoors whenever possible. He paints the South Texas landscape—dusty terrain dotted with low brush and cactus in bright sunlight—using beautifully realistic colors that are equally muted and vibrant.

Noe Perez is a master at capturing the beauty and essence of South Texas from San Antonio to the Rio Grande.

SELECTED BIOGRAPHICAL AND CAREER HIGHLIGHTS

1979 BS, Civil Engineering, A&I University, Kingsville

2009 and 2011 Honorable Mention for Artistic Excellence, Jury's Top 50, *Salon International Art Show*, Greenhouse Gallery, San Antonio

2010 Included in *Texas Traditions*, Fresno Fine Art Publications, LLC

2015 Commissioned to paint the King Ranch Main House to celebrate the Centennial Anniversary of the home

Resides in Corpus Christi, Texas

SELECTED EXHIBITIONS

2006–08 *Night of Artists*, Briscoe Western Art Museum, San Antonio

2008–11 *Salon International*, Greenhouse Gallery, San Antonio

2010 *Texas Traditions*, Heritage Gallery, Dallas and Insight Gallery, Fredericksburg

2010–11 Alamo Kiwanis Show, San Antonio

2012 *Contemporary Texas Regionalists*, traveled: Haley Memorial Library & History Center, Midland; Gage Hotel, Marathon

2013 *Restless Heart: Contemporary Texas Regionalism*, San Angelo Museum of Fine Arts, San Angelo (catalog)

2013 *Celebrating the Regionalist Legacy in Texas Art*, William Reaves Fine Art and the San Angelo Museum of Fine Arts at the Gage Hotel, Marathon

2013 *Holidays at the Haley*, Haley Memorial Library & History Center, Midland

2014–15 *Painting in the Texas Tradition*, traveled: Turner House, Dallas; Pearl Fincher Museum of Fine Arts, Spring (catalog)
2015 *Ties that Bind: Contemporary Texas Regionalism*, Turner House, Dallas
2015 *Texas Visions: Contemporary Texas Regionalism*, Nave Museum, Victoria
2015 *As Far as the Eye Can See: 100 Years of Texas Art*, Two Allen Center, Houston
2016 *Texas Landscapes*, Nave Museum, Victoria (catalog)

SELECTED PUBLIC COLLECTIONS

Icon Bank, Galleria Houston
King Ranch, Kingsville
Kleberg National Bank, Kingsville
San Jacinto Title Co., Corpus Christi
University of Texas at San Antonio

Jeri Salter (b. 1955, Richmond, Virginia)

Though originally from Virginia, Jeri Salter has lived all over Texas—in Houston, McAllen, Plano, Lago Vista, and, currently, Round Rock. A self-taught artist, Salter honed her skills over the years through various classes and workshops, focusing her talent on pastel landscapes.

Her paintings often parallel images from early Texas artist Frank Reaugh as she derives her inspiration from the vast beauty in nature, highlighting the open skies and rolling plains of the Texas landscape. Most recently, she has found similar beauty in rural buildings and roadways.

Salter describes her landscapes as having remnants of humanity, captured in the scenes that feature derelict buildings and worn dirt roads. In painting these ordinary scenes, she tries to convey an appreciation of the natural beauty and the emotional sense of "searching" evoked therein.

SELECTED BIOGRAPHICAL AND CAREER HIGHLIGHTS

1983–84 Glassell School of Art, Houston
1994–95 Collin County Community College, Plano
2002–present Member, Central Texas Pastel Society
2005–08 President, Central Texas Pastel Society

2007–present Member, Austin Pastel Society

2009 Best in Show, *Austin Pastel Society Miniature Show*, Austin

2009, 2012, 2015 Best in Show, *Central Texas Pastel Society Membership Competition*, Cultural Activities Center, Temple

2010 Mark Chapman Award, Best in Show, *Artwalk Competition*, Fayetteville, Texas

2010, 2012 Pastel Second Place, *Western Art Show*, Phippen Museum, Prescott, Arizona

2011, 2014 Pastel First Place, *Western Art Show*, Phippen Museum, Prescott, Arizona

Resides in Round Rock, Texas

SELECTED EXHIBITIONS

2004–05 *Wildflower Art Show*, Salado

2004–05 *Art Walk*, Georgetown

2005–06 *Artist Harvest Facet Show*, Austin

2006 *Holiday Show*, Lady Bird Johnson Wildflower Center, Austin

2007–09 *Holiday Show*, Laguna Gloria Museum, Austin

2008–09 *Texas Wild Bunch*, Professional Artists' Show, Kerrville

2009 *Austin Pastel Society Miniature Show*, Austin

2009 *Central Texas Pastel Society Membership Competition*, Cultural Activities Center, Temple

2010 *Artwalk Competition*, Fayetteville

2010–11 *Main Street Festival*, Fort Worth

2010–11 *Fiesta Show*, San Antonio

2010–11 *Bayou City Downtown and Memorial Show*, Houston

2010–11 *Cottonwood Art Festival*, Richardson

2010–11 *Art City Austin Show*, Austin

2010–11 *Artscape Show*, Dallas Arboretum, Dallas

2010–12, 2014 *Western Art Show*, Phippen Museum, Prescott, Arizona

2011 Featured Artist, *Fayetteville Artwalk*, Fayetteville

2012 *Central Texas Pastel Society Membership Competition*, Cultural Activities Center, Temple

2012 *Contemporary Texas Regionalists*, traveled: Haley Memorial Library & History Center, Midland; Gage Hotel, Marathon

2013 *Restless Heart: Contemporary Texas Regionalism*, San Angelo Museum of Fine Arts, San Angelo (catalog)

2013 *Celebrating the Regionalist Legacy in Texas Art*, William Reaves Fine Art and the San Angelo Museum of Fine Arts at the Gage Hotel, Marathon

2013 *Holidays at the Haley*, Haley Memorial Library & History Center, Midland

2014–15 *Painting in the Texas Tradition*, traveled: Turner House, Dallas; Pearl Fincher Museum of Fine Arts, Spring (catalog)

2015 *Ties that Bind: Contemporary Texas Regionalism*, Turner House, Dallas

2015 Solo, *On the Trail of Frank Reaugh: The Pastel Journals of Jeri Salter*, William Reaves Fine Art, Houston

2015 *Central Texas Pastel Society Membership Competition*, Cultural Activities Center, Temple

2015 *Texas Visions: Contemporary Texas Regionalism*, Nave Museum, Victoria

2015 *As Far as the Eye Can See: 100 Years of Texas Art*, Two Allen Center, Houston

SELECTED PUBLIC COLLECTIONS

BNSF Railroad Collection, Fort Worth

Happy State Bank, Amarillo

Icon Bank, Galleria, Houston

Icon Bank, Sugarland

San Angelo Museum of Fine Arts, San Angelo

Erik Sprohge (b. 1932, Riga, Latvia)

Erik Sprohge spent his early childhood in Germany before coming to Houston with his family in 1937. At sixteen, he was a student of Lowell Collins and Robert Preusser at the Museum School, Museum of Fine Arts, Houston. He received a degree in architecture from Rice Institute and won the William Ward Watkin Traveling Fellowship, enabling him to travel extensively throughout Europe.

While in the US Army, Sprohge worked as a part-time illustrator for special services. Upon his return, he began doing architectural rendering, a specialization he continued until 2007. He studied painting at the Institute Allende in San Miguel de Allende, Mexico under Fred Samuelson before becoming design partner in Converse, Sprohge, & Cox Architects in Houston.

Sprohge studied under Philip Renteria at the Glassell School of Art and has been active in the Art League of Houston and the Watercolor Art Society. As a watercolorist, Sprohge's works reflect actual or remembered scenes that, while realistically rendered, portray the spirit behind the reality.

SELECTED BIOGRAPHICAL AND CAREER HIGHLIGHTS

1938 Moved to Houston
1938–48 Museum School, Museum of Fine Arts, Houston
1949–54 BS Architecture, Rice Institute, Houston
1955–57 Served in US Army
1957–2007 Architectural Rendering
1961 Instituto Allende, San Miguel de Allende, Mexico
1962 First Prize, Great Southern Life Insurance
1964–72 Design Partner, Converse, Sprohge, & Cox Architects, Houston
1966 Fred Ealand Memorial Award, Art League of Houston
1981 Glassell School of Art, Houston
1999–present Signature Elite Membership, Watercolor Art Society-Houston (WAS-H)
1999–present 43 Awards including 12 First Prizes, Watercolor Art Society-Houston (WAS-H)
2005 Lifetime Achievement Award as an Early Texas Artist, Center for the Advancement and Study of Early Texas Art (CASETA)
2009 First Prize, Houston Grand Opera, Houston
Resides in Houston, Texas

SELECTED EXHIBITIONS

1960 Dreyer Gallery, Houston, Texas
1962 *Christmas Billboard Design*, Great Southern Life Insurance Company
1964 Nobler Gallery Westbury Square, Houston
1966 *Dimension Houston Show*, Art League of Houston
1969 Lantern Lane Gallery, Houston

1974 Solo, Jack Meier Gallery, Houston
1988, 1991 Mother Dog Studios, Houston
1997 Solo, Lowell Collins Gallery, Houston
1999–present Participation in monthly and special shows, Watercolor Art Society-Houston (WAS-H)
2002–06 *Annual International Show*, Watercolor Art Society-Houston (WAS-H)
2005 *Rice Institute and The Visual Arts in Houston 1900–1960*, Houston
2006 Solo, William Tower Gallery, Houston
2006 *Early Houston Artists in Houston Collections*, Heritage Society, Houston
2009 *Midsummer Nights Dream Painting Competition*, Houston Grand Opera, Houston
2009 Solo, *Inward—Outward*, Gallery M Squared, Houston
2011, 2013 *Annual International Show*, Watercolor Art Society-Houston (WAS-H)

COLLECTIONS

Numerous private collectors

Debbie Stevens (b. 1955, Stillwater, Oklahoma)

Debbie Stevens quickly discovered her love for art and pursued it in her studies, graduating summa cum laude from the University of Texas at San Antonio with a bachelor of fine arts degree with a concentration in painting.

She has studied landscape, still life, and figure with contemporary masters Dalhart Windberg, Robert A. Johnson, Scott Burdick, and Jeff Legg and has attended workshops in bird photography with nationally acclaimed wildlife photographers Jim Nieger and Arthur Morris. Stevens is a signature member of the Oil Painters of America, signature member of the Society of Animal Artists, a member of the International Guild of Realism, and a member of the Contemporary Texas Regionalists.

Stevens states that her work is created with a devotion to traditional realism. She looks for subjects in nature and the environment, searching to capture their particular properties of texture, transparency, reflection, and color.

Her intense passion for birds has grown from visiting zoos and interacting with endangered species. She has conducted in-depth research and tracked fly-routes to accurately depict behaviors during spring and fall migrations. It is her sincere desire for viewers to experience the wonderment of birds in their natural habitat through her work.

SELECTED BIOGRAPHICAL AND CAREER HIGHLIGHTS

2004 BFA, University of Texas at San Antonio

Signature Member, Oil Painters of America and Society of Animal Artists

Member, International Guild of Realism

2004 Naima and Joseph Abraham Memorial Award, Second Place Painting, *Arts International*, El Paso

2005 Award of Excellence, *14th Annual National Juried Exhibition*, Oil Painters of America

2010 First Place, Wildlife Competition, *The Artists Magazine*

2010 Third Place, "21 Over 31" Artists to Watch, *Southwest Art Magazine*

2014 Fine Art Connoisseur Award, *54th Annual Art and the Animal Exhibition,* Society of Animal Artists, the Wildlife Experience, Parker, Colorado

Resides in Cypress, Texas

SELECTED EXHIBITIONS

2004, 2006, 2008, 2010–11, 2013 *Salon International*, Greenhouse Gallery, San Antonio

2005, 2007–10, 2013 *Annual National Juried Exhibition*, Oil Painters of America, gallery venues nationwide

2005 *Central Regional Exhibition*, Oil Painters of America

2005 *First Annual Juried Exhibition*, International Guild of Realism, Pan America Art Gallery, Brownsville

2008 *Western Regional Exhibition*, Oil Painters of America, Devine Galleries, Coeur d'Arlene, Idaho

2008 *Third Annual Juried Exhibition*, International Guild of Realism, Scottsdale Fine Art, Scottsdale, Arizona

2009–10 *49th Annual Art and the Animal Exhibition and Tour*, Society of Animal Artists, Premiere: Rolling Hills Wildlife Adventure, Salina, Kansas; Tour: Dunnegan Gallery of Art, Bolivar, Missouri; Ward Museum of Wildfowl Art, Salisbury, Maryland (in conjunction with the 40th Anniversary Ward World Championship Wildfowl Carving Competition, Roland E. Powell Convention Center, Ocean City, Maryland)

2010–11 *50th Annual Art and the Animal Exhibition and Tour*, Society of Animal Artists, Premiere: San Diego Natural History Museum, San Diego; Encore: The Wildlife Experience, Parker, Colorado; Tour: Dunnegan Gallery of Art, Bolivar, Missouri; Sam Noble Oklahoma Museum of Natural History, Norman, Oklahoma

2010–12 *Birds in Art*, Exhibition: Leigh Yawkey Woodson Museum, Wausau, Wisconsin; National Tour: Museum of the Gulf Coast, Port Arthur, Texas; Newington Cropsey Foundation, Hastings-on-the-Hudson, New York; Wendell Gilley Museum, Southwest Harbor, Maine; Michelson Museum of Art, Marshall, Texas

2011 *Sixth Annual Juried Exhibition*, International Guild of Realism, Sage Creek Gallery, Santa Fe, New Mexico

2012 *Contemporary Texas Regionalists*, traveled: Haley Memorial Library & History Center, Midland; Gage Hotel, Marathon

2013 *Restless Heart: Contemporary Texas Regionalism*, San Angelo Museum of Fine Arts, San Angelo (catalog)

2013 *Celebrating the Regionalist Legacy in Texas Art*, William Reaves Fine Art and the San Angelo Museum of Fine Arts at the Gage Hotel, Marathon

2013 *Holidays at the Haley*, Haley Memorial Library & History Center, Midland

2013–14 *Birds in Art*, Exhibition: Leigh Yawkey Woodson Museum, Wausau, Wisconsin; National Tour: Heritage Center, State Historical Society of North Dakota, Bismarck; Steamboat Art Museum, Steamboat Springs, Colorado; Michelson Museum of Art, Marshall, Texas

2014–15 *Painting in the Texas Tradition*, traveled: Turner House, Dallas; Pearl Fincher Museum of Fine Arts, Spring (catalog)

2014–15 *54th Annual Art and the Animal Exhibition and Tour*, Society of Animal Artists, Premier: The Wildlife Experience, Parker, Colorado; Tour: Hiram Blauvelt Art Museum, Oradell, New Jersey; Dunnegan Gallery of Art, Bolivar, Missouri; National Sporting Library and Museum, Middleburg, Virginia

2014–16 *Birds in Art,* Exhibition: Leigh Yawkey Woodson Museum, Wausau, Wisconsin; National Tour: Museum of the Gulf Coast, Port Arthur, Texas; Arizona-Sonora Desert Museum, Tucson; Wildling Museum, Solvang, California; Newington-Cropsey Foundation, Hastings-on-Hudson, New York, Gilcrease Museum, Tulsa, Oklahoma

2015 *Ties that Bind: Contemporary Texas Regionalism*, Turner House, Dallas

2015 *Texas Visions: Contemporary Texas Regionalism*, Nave Museum, Victoria

SELECTED PUBLIC COLLECTIONS

Dr. Philips Hospital, Orlando, Florida
Holmes Regional Medical, Melbourne, Florida
Memorial Hermann TIRR, Houston
Memorial Hermann Hospital, Sugar Land
Memorial Hermann Heart and Vascular Institute, Houston
Memorial Hermann Ambulatory Care Center, Houston
Thibodaux Regional Medical, Thibodaux, Louisiana

William Young (b. 1952, Abilene, Texas)

William Young paints full-time at his studio in the Piney Woods of East Texas in Palestine. His formal art training included drawing and printmaking courses at the University of Dallas, East Texas State University, and Stephen F. Austin State University. Young also studied painting with Ancel Nunn and helped in the printing of several of Nunn's stone-pulled lithographs.

Young's paintings, etchings, and drawings all have a surreal undercurrent derived from a combination of experience painting under Nunn's tutelage and his personal inclination for the enigmatic and often strange folklore of Texas. A variety of his works are created as a visual homage to these Lone Star folk stories, while other works are created purely from lyrics of songs that inspire him.

Young's first art show was as at Temple Emanu-El Art Festival in 1976 where his etching, *The Last Letter*, was judged best-in-show by a panel of judges that included Harry Parker, then Director of the Dallas Museum of Art. Since then, Young has pursued both a fine art and commercial art career. His paintings, etchings, and drawings are included in many private collections.

SELECTED BIOGRAPHICAL AND CAREER HIGHLIGHTS

University of Dallas, Dallas
East Texas State University, Commerce
Stephen F. Austin State University, Nacogdoches
2009 Dallas Nine Award, Dallas
2009 Featured Artist, Article, *D Magazine*, Dallas
2010 Finalist, Hunting Art Prize Competition, Houston
2013 Finalist, Hunting Art Prize Competition, Houston
Resides in Palestine, Texas

SELECTED EXHIBITIONS

2005 Tyler Museum of Art, Tyler
2005 Museum for East Texas Culture, Palestine
2006 Trinity River Arts Center, Dallas
2007 *Texas Five*, Museum for East Texas Culture, Palestine
2007 *Then and Now*, Texas State University, San Marcos
2007–09 *Cherry Spring Arts Festival*, Cherry Spring
2009 *Etchings and Dreamscapes*, Longview Museum of Fine Art, Longview
2010 *Invitational Western Art Show and Sale*, Panhandle-Plains Historical Museum, Canyon
2010 *Hunting Art Prize Exhibition*, Houston
2012 *Contemporary Texas Regionalists*, traveled: Haley Memorial Library & History Center, Midland; Gage Hotel, Marathon
2013 *Restless Heart: Contemporary Texas Regionalism*, San Angelo Museum of Fine Arts, San Angelo (catalog)

2013 *Celebrating the Regionalist Legacy in Texas Art*, William Reaves Fine Art and the San Angelo Museum of Fine Arts at the Gage Hotel, Marathon

2013 *Hunting Art Prize Exhibition*, Houston

2013 *Holidays at the Haley*, Haley Memorial Library & History Center, Midland

2014 *Painting in the Texas Tradition*, Turner House, Dallas

SELECTED PUBLIC COLLECTIONS

Silver Eagle Distributors, Houston

St. Arnold's Brewery Mural, Houston

CANADIAN
RED
White
Pease
RED
BRAZOS
TRINITY
Cedar Cr.
Sabine
Paluxy
COLORADO
Delaware
Neches
TRINITY
BRAZOS
PECOS
San Saba
San Gabriel
Devils
Llano
Little
Big Sandy Cr.
Pedernales
San Jacinto
Guadalupe
COLORADO
Buffalo Bayou
San Marcos
Sabinal
San Antonio
Trinity Bay
Galveston Bay
Frio
Nueces
Matagorda Bay
Aransas Bay
Santa Gertrudis Cr.
RIO GRANDE

INDEX OF RIVERS

Aransas Bay, 98
Brazos River, 1, 16, 23, 56, 73, 82, 87, 89, 100, 109
Buffalo Bayou, 29, 30, 31, 74, 75, 103
Colorado River, 58, 66, 67, 68, 69, 70
Delaware River, 78 (McKittrick Canyon)
Devils River, 60, 61, 83
Frio River, 8, 63 (North Little Creek), 64
Guadalupe River, 6, 9, 28, 37, 71, 80, 104
Gulf Coast near Matagorda Bay, 13, 84, 107
Coastal Marshes in Harris County, 106
Llano River, 81 (Threadgill Creek)
Neches River, 93
Nueces River, 92, 5 (Pulliam Creek), 94 (Pulliam Creek), 95, 96 (Santa Gertrudis Creek)
Paluxy River, 34
Pease River, 90
Pecos River, 102
Pedernales River, 22, 37
Red River, 108
Rio Grande, 62, 65, 72, 99
Sabine River, 33 (Big Sandy Creek), 85
San Antonio River, 24, 26, 27
San Gabriel River, 101
San Jacinto River, 86 (Houston Ship Channel)
San Marcos River, 25
San Saba River, 88
Trinity Bay, 105
Trinity River, 32 (Cedar Creek), 35, 57, 77
Unidentified River, 36
White River, 91